GUILTY

Written by

Dr. Dennis Straub

(D. Min., M. Div.)

TABLE OF CONTENTS

Chapter 1

INTRODUCTION

It would seem odd to write a doctoral thesis on "sin", because there are literally hundreds of thousands of books written over the centuries about some aspect of sin; yet there remains considerable confusion about what sin is and how the church and, ultimately, society should define sin. When I was in college, studying structural engineering, the professor told the class about the common, accepted practice of the day that columns had strength according to size and not shape. He created a project to prove a rectangular column had different structural properties than a square column. His thesis changed, universally, how columns were designed.

The church has had a mindset that sin is just sin. Society has adopted a general view that there may be big sins and little sins, but the shape (or nature) of sin is, for the most part, unimportant. In this study, "society" is defined as a social order founded by Christians having a Christian-consciousness, such as the United States of America, Canada or European countries. This is in sharp contrast to a Muslim society where, under Shria Law, there is no concept of "sin" and, therefore, no need of a savior. In addition, a Buddhist or Hindu society where the primary belief of reincarnation negates the need of sin-consciousness, the concept of "sin" is vastly different from the understanding of Jewish and Christian societies.

The spread of Christianity from Jerusalem in the first century AD to all corners of the world has always had Hebraic roots. The establishment of the Ten Commandments Yahweh gave to Moses, as recorded in the Exodus narrative, is always found in every Christian community. Therefore, no study of "sin" can exclude a serious examination of the concept of sin in the Old Testament. Though this study does not debate Continuance-Discontinuance theology, that is what is retained and what is not retained from the Old Testament into the New Testament, nevertheless, current laws concerning acts such as murder have a Mosaic foundation. Since thoughts influence behavior, and behavior influences action, and action influences lifestyle, an understanding of sin is critical in understanding the reason people act in the manner that they do. This study has not an emphasis on psychology or counseling, but rather a study on understanding the Mosaic concept of sin-consciousness, how that concept was foundational in the Early Church and is relevant in today's church. No activity in life characterizes men and women more than "sin". Few people, when asked to examine their lives, truthfully begin to claim their academic achievements, their career achievements, their family relations, their wealth or their worldview; but begin to immediately turn their thoughts to those times when they believed they sinned. "If only the clock of time could be turned back" is often the moan as they sigh over the things they desperately would like to change, like a teacher erasing what was written on the chalkboard.

Yet most Christians were told at the point of their conversion that Jesus died for the sins of the world and if they confess Christ, all their sins would be wiped away, like the schoolteacher cleaning the chalkboard. If indeed that is true, why did Jesus say that blasphemy against the Holy Spirit was a sin not forgivable (Mk 3:28-29)? Why does the Lord's Prayer end with the admonition that if we do not forgive other men their trespasses that our Heavenly Father will not forgive our trespasses (Mt 6:14-15)? Church history records how Catholic, Lutherans and Calvinists all participated in the drowning of thousands of Anabaptists because they rejected full water baptism, believing that they were doing the work of God. If intentional drowning can be considered murder, and murder considered as sin, and since these Catholics, Lutherans and Calvinists remained unrepentant, what of their sin? Do we have any evidence that Christ automatically erases our sins? Protestants scorn the Catholics for their system of penance; that your sin is forgiven if you only repeat a few "Hail Marys". Too many have used the penance system to erase their guilt, but not change their sinful lifestyle.

Having established that a Christian indeed can have trespasses not forgiven, the century-old religious concept that if we just confess the Lordship of Christ that Jesus wipes away all our sin suddenly stands on faulty ground. In no way am I proposing to limit the graciousness of the saving power of the blood of Christ. Rather, the notion that salvation from sin is somehow automatic, that we all die in Christ and go to heaven, we all get a mansion (Jn. 14:2) and we all come, one day, back to reign with Christ as kings and priests (Rev. 5:10), is much more magical than theological. Indeed, there are those who will get a mansion, great rewards and will return to rule. However, scripture leads me to believe it will be only those who live righteously and walk in obedience to what the Lord calls them to do. There is no concept of a free lunch in scripture: all the parables of the Lord are based on reward for faith-infused, righteous conduct, not on jumping on a band wagon of respectability. If there are rewards to be won, by simple deduction, one reaches the conclusion that not all will receive rewards. For many Christians, the old sacrificial system was messy and they are glad they do not have to participate in it, however, the deliberate throwing away of the knowledge of the sacrificial system leaves the believer with a void of understanding, and a lack of appreciation of the seriousness of their sin. Church history reveals that the church has always been the strongest when it has a high regard for sin. The modern church has become very acceptable because it has lost its sin-consciousness, it no longer is a voice against abortion or homosexuality, but has become a feel-good religious club. Today, Christians step into a marriage covenant, only to later throw the marriage away often because it does not meet their selfish needs. They have little or no concept that they stand as a covenant-breaker before the Lord. In addition, divorce is seen as a sin no worse than cheating on your income tax or speeding. Some believers break financial covenants, such as refusing to honor credit card debts or employment contracts, thinking God is always there to automatically erase their errors. We have come to a crisis of cheap grace in our churches, and we break our covenants without regard to the individual spiritual impact or the corporal impact of church, community and country.

That is why I believe a church's fundamental understanding of the concept of sin impacts their members' spiritual life and social interaction, as their choices influence for both good and evil, both within and without the church environment. These choices influence the very destiny of the church. I have studied the original languages, as it pertains to the concept of sin in both the Old and New Testaments, because I desired to find out how a personal concept of sin by believers today is determining the course of the Church of Jesus Christ universally.

In the early 1980s, I was involved in an engineering project where a company was given a government grant to fabricate a large steel windmill that would power an oil well pump. The reasoning was that over time, wind power would be cheaper than electricity to extract the oil. The engineers naturally looked at historical Dutch windmill designs and soon discovered that though they had a fair measure of efficiency, when they were enlarged, the efficiency dramatically fell. The research that followed required the engineers to throw away all they knew about windmill blade design and, by using modern computer wind analogy from the aeronautical industry, they developed a very different set of blades. So it has been with this study; I have had to put my former understanding of sin aside and search for new definitions.

There are countless books about sin. Puritans, such as Rutherford, created classics on sin, and they wrote to convince people not to sin; it always was from an English understanding of sin. This study is not concerned about the consequences or horror of sin; but to discover how the ancient Hebrews understood the words they used to describe sin, and then to discover how Christ and the early Church understood these words also.

The primary purpose of this study is to search for the use of Hebrew words for sin and their relevant Greek words, as found in the LXX and NT. Once I have examined the words for sin in both testaments, then I will consider how God views sin, the role of Christ as High Priest, the atonement and the impact of obedience, as it affects the believer, the church and the advancement or retreat of the church.

Chapter 2
PROBLEMS CONTRIBUTING TO A SKEWED VIEW OF SIN

E lwell states that sin is a riddle, a mystery, a reality that defies definition and comprehension.[1] I do not completely agree. Though defining sin is not an easy task, the gift of revelation given to men means that to the person who diligently seeks truth, sin does not need to remain a riddle or mystery. There is no "super" word for sin that blankets all forms of violation against God, his laws or his creation. The word "sin" does not exist in the original languages of Hebrew and Greek, but comes into Old English as "synn" from the Vulgate, a Latin word that means "**guilty**". [2] Many commentaries and lexicons define the words for "sin" using the other words in the list, as if they are in fact similes. Strong's concordance defines "sin" as ignorance, inattention,

---

1   Walter A. Elwell, *Baker Theological Dictionary of the Bible.* (Grand Rapids: Baker Books, 1996), 736.

2   Carl F. H. Henry, *Baker's Dictionary of Christian Ethics.* (Grand Rapids: Baker Books, 1973), 620.

missing the mark, iniquity, rebellion, trespassing, disobedience, guilt, wickedness, trouble and offense.[3] If the reader then looks up the word "offence", it references to lead astray, crime, fault, to be deceived or to sin ignorantly. Strong's also defines "iniquity" as evil, fault, sin, punishment and mischief, and defines "evil" as bad, affliction, hurtful, mischief, wicked and wrong. The Brown-Driver-Briggs Hebrew and English Lexicon defines the Hebrew word "asham" as an offence, a trespass, guilt, wrongdoing or iniquity.[4] The Hebrew word "pasha" usually translated as "transgression" is also defined as guilt and defilement.[5] The Hebrew word "hata" is usually translated as "sin" but is defined as a wrong, a mistake, missing the mark, bring into guilt, uncleanness and an offence.[6] The problem that arises is what is called circular theology, one word defines a second word and the second word is defined by a third word and so on, until the last word in the list is defined by the first word.

---

3   *The New Strong's Concise Concordance & Vine's Concise Dictionary of the Bible.* (Nashville, Tennessee: Thomas Nelson Inc., 1997), 344.

4   F. Brown, S. Driver, C. Briggs, *The Brown-Driver-Briggs Hebrew and English Lexicon*, (Peabody, Mass.: Hendrickson, 2003), 79.

5   Ibid, BDB, 833.

6   Brown, S. Driver, C. Briggs, *The Brown-Driver-Briggs Hebrew and English Lexicon*, (Peabody, Mass.: Hendrickson, 2003), 308.

The Eskimos of Northern Canada have over 20 words for snow, because snow is a major part of their survival; it defines their environment. In a similar fashion, the Hebrews had over 20 words for different kinds of sin, because it defined their environment. The type of sin determined the type of restitution and sacrifice that had to be offered. Both the Eskimos and the Hebrews had small vocabularies; there are less than 3,000 root words in Hebrew, compared to over 25,000 words in English. That meant that every word had a well-defined meaning.

The Hebrews used poetry, idioms, lists and repetition. The Psalmist often used repetition of poetry for the sake of emphasis, such as "the mountains skipped like rams, and the little hills like lambs" (Ps. 114:4). It must be interpreted as an expression of joy. Joel prophesied that, "The sun shall be turned into darkness, and the moon into blood, before the great and the terrible day of the Lord."(Joel 2:31). This is a Hebrew idiom that warns of a coming great slaughter, but has nothing to do with the physical sun or moon. When Nehemiah returned, he carefully noted all of the items brought back from Babylon such as horses, mules, camels and asses (Neh. 7:69). Theologians have no difficulty distinguishing between these animals, but have difficulty distinguishing between iniquity, sin, wickedness and rebellion. When theologians consider the verse, "We have sinned, and have committed iniquity, and have done wickedness, and have rebelled, even by departing from your precepts and from your judgments" (Dan 9:5); they argue that the words sin, iniquity, wickedness and rebellion all mean the same thing. However, these words are not similes, but rather a list of very specific sins.

To complicate matters worse, translators often did not strictly adhere to specific words for each Hebrew word; resulting in a literary license, as if one word seemed to sound better than another word. The Hebrew word "ra", means "evil", but was translated into English as wicked (Gen. 13:13), as mischief (Ex. 32:22) and as adversity (Ps. 94:13). There also is no consistency with the LXX, for the word "evil" was translated as bad, missing the mark and faithless. Concerning the King James, the Greek word "wicked" is "asebes"; but translators also translated it as "trouble" (2 Pt. 2:7), "lawlessness" (2 Thes. 2:3), "iniquity" (Acts 2:23) and "evil" (Matt. 21:41). If you had ten different pieces of fruit, you could put them in a bowl and call it "bowl of fruit". However, a banana, apple, orange, kiwi, lemon, pomegranate, cherries, blueberries and pear are very different; so different that it is a wonder they are all called fruits. The same is with sin, there are many fruits of sin that are wildly different, yet have one thing in common: they each have the power to send a person to hell. If you asked your wife to bake you an apple pie and she used bananas instead, irrespective of how well she made the pie, a banana pie will never taste like an apple pie. Yet the church interchanges words for sin as if they all mean the same.

The problem is that the Christian definition of sin has been tossed about since the time of the Church Fathers. The Christian leaders, through the centuries, have been **guilty** of not clearly identifying the biblical concept of sin.

Chapter 3

BRIEF HISTORICAL CONSIDERATIONS OF THE CONCEPT OF SIN

I t is not the intent of this study to give a detailed summary
of how Christians through the centuries have defined
sin, but merely to point out that there has been an evolution
of how sin was thought of. The concept that Christians did
not have to obey all the Jewish laws is clearly stated in Acts
15; but controversy has continued through the centuries
as to what is borrowed and what is not. The doctrine of
Continuance and Discontinuance has attempted to address
this problem through the centuries. Certainly, Christians
do not prepare their food like Jews (with the exception
of Messianic Christians and Seventh Day Adventists).
However, as a society, we have adopted Mosaic practices
such as the Sabbath, the death penalty and views about
incest and homosexuality.

1.   Early Church Fathers and their Concept of Sin

The Babylonian captivity dramatically impacted the mindset of Israel and the successive captivity of Rome also impacted the mindset of the Early Church. In 174 BC, Antichus IV invaded Israel and, in an attempt to Hellenize the Jews, He made a proclamation that no Jew could read the Torah, no Jew could rest on the Sabbath, no Jew could be circumcised and all Jewish feasts were outlawed. Antiochus took on the name "Epiphanies", which means "manifest", thus declaring himself as "a god in the flesh" and required all Jews to worship him as a god.[7] When Antiochus ordered swine to be sacrificed on the altar at Jerusalem, an old priest by the name of Mattathais killed the representative of Antiochus and touched off the Maccabean War. The Jews fought the Greeks so fiercely that they finally gave the Jews the right of worship. When the Romans came, they had heard of the fierceness of the Maccabean War and, desiring peace, did not intrude religiously in Jewish affairs. In fact, Herod had work done on the temple site for 40 years in order to please the Jews. However, the Early Church quickly spread throughout the Roman Empire into cities where Caesar was worshipped as a god in the flesh. Rouselle argues that Caesar Augustus had banned unequal marriages with his laws

---

7   Jack Finegan, *Handbook of Biblical Chronology*. (NJ: Princeton University Press, 1964), 251.

"Lex Julia" and "Lex Papia Poppaea". These laws imposed severe restrictions on a Roman's choice of wife, in order to prevent men from marrying beneath themselves. Sons and daughters of senators were forbidden to marry slaves, prostitutes, freed persons, actors and those condemned for adultery.[8] This is significant when more than 60 percent of Rome were slaves. In addition, any child born outside a legitimate lawful marriage had no legal ties with the father. The Roman was obliged by law to marry, however, he was free to choose his wife, but was not bound to remain faithful to his wife. There were three crimes: incest, stuprum and adultery, which could lead to a man losing his position in his family. Stuprum occurred when a man had sex with a young boy, sex with a young girl from a good family or sex with a widow.[9] Since many of the converts into the Early Church were slaves, Early Church fathers struggled to define sin in a Roman society where the emperor was worshipped as "god in the flesh", and where temple prostitution, concubinage and slavery were everyday realities. Tertullian, writing his "Apology" in 197 AD, mentions that child sacrifices were still part of the "Saturn" cult. Though banned by Rome, this Libyan-Punic cult had originated in Carthage but continued

---

8   Aline Rouselle, *Porneia : On Desire and the Body in Antiquity.*
      (Oxford: Basel Blackwell Inc., 1988), 78.

9   Ibid, Rouselle, 79.

to be practiced.[10] According to Diodorus Siculus' Library of History, Kronos was the recipient of child sacrifices at Carthage, a tradition traced back to the Phoenicians at Crete in the Early Iron Age. In addition, according the Philo, Kronos (time) sacrificed his only son to his father Ouranos (heaven).[11] Here is a practice that, though fully purged from the Jews, was still alive among the Gentiles.

Feinberg states the first century church fathers, such as Justin Martyr in his "First Apology" and Irenaeus in his "Adverus haeresis" writings, offer reflection on the question of interrelationships between the testaments.[12] Therefore, in a time when the New Testament scriptures were yet to be canonized, they struggled to define what parts of the Law of Moses to retain and what parts to reject. Their acceptance and rejection would define their concept of sin. Christ, Paul, James and John never spoke against slavery; something the modern church considers a great violation of the human spirit. In addition, the church remained under tremendous persecution and due to the persecution, the critical sin of the time was denial of the faith to save one's life. There has been considerable, historical debate regarding what is meant to

---

10   Ibid, Rouselle,109.

11   Mark Smith, *The Early History of God.* (San Francisco: Harper & Row Publishers, 1990), 135.

12   John S Feinberg, *Continuity and Discontinuity*, (Westchester, Illinois: Crossway Books, 1988), 19.

be apostate. The Novatians quoted Hebrews10:38; "and if he shrinks back, my soul has no pleasure in him, but we are not those who shrink back to perdition." Hughes argues that the Novatians in the 3rd Century denied any place for repentance and restoration to those who lapsed under persecution.[13] The Greek word for "perdition" is "apoleia", which means "destruction", and was used especially in regards to "eternal punishment for the wicked" (Mt 7:13).[14] Certainly persecution at the time was severe, and no one would suggest the Christians volunteer to be martyrs. For Hughes, it was not a question of a passive falling away but a deliberate rebellious desertion from their faith.[15]

The 1st century Church sprang up mainly among slaves, who saw Christianity as an eternal reward for enduring the sinful practices their masters placed on them. It was a time when Augustine would write the classic "City of God" as Christians yearned for a better life, free from sin. For venial sins, Augustine defined evil as a privation of good, that is nothing evil exists in itself. He used the example a drink cannot be sweet and sour at the same time and place,

---

13   P.E. Hughes, *Commentary on the Epistle to the Hebrews.* (Grand Rapids: Eerdmans, 1977), 419.

14   Frederick William Danker, *A Greek-English Lexicon of the New Testament and other Early Christian Literature*, 3d ed, (Chicago: University of Chicago, 2000), 127.

15   P. E. Hughes, *Commentary on the Epistle to the Hebrews.* (Grand Rapids: Eerdmans, 1977), 145.

whereas good can exist without evil, but evil cannot exist without good. Without good, evil has no mode in which to exist.[16] Yet for original sin, Augustine believed that baptism cleansed of original sin, but that infants also share in the actual sins of their forefathers, at least as far back as two or three generations.[17] Therefore, Augustine understood sin entered at birth as a result of the sins of previous generations, but in defining evil as the opposite of good, he struggled to define the concept of sin.

2.   The Medieval Concept of Sin

Pope Gregory (590 – 604) decreed that Augustine was an infallible teacher; what was for Augustine, conjecture, became certainty for Gregory. Augustine speculated on purgatory, but Gregory affirmed the existence of purgatory, developed the doctrine of purgatory and taught that the living can help those in purgatory.[18] This doctrine meant that Christians left this world for a place of purifying, but living relatives could speed their progress from purgatory to heaven by making financial contributions to the church.

---

16   Geoffrey W. Bromiley, *Historical Theology: An Introduction.* (Grand Rapids: Eerdmans, 1978), 110.

17   Ibid, Bromiley, 112.

18   Justo Gonzalez, *The Story of Christianity*, Vol 1, *The Early Church to the Dawn of the Reformation.* (San Francisco: Harper Collins Publishers, 1984), 247.

Dante Alighieri (1265 –1321) wrote of the seven unpardonable, deadly sins in his book, "Divine Comedy", as pride, covetousness, lust, anger, gluttony, envy and sloth.[19] However bad these sins are, there is no scriptural evidence to support his writings were factual or mere fantasy. However, the Roman Catholic Church would develop a well-defined theology of mortal sins and venial sins. Souls, which are completely pure at death, were allowed to enter heaven, but others, which are not pure, and were in need of cleansing, had to go to a place of purging to purge away their venial sins.[20] Therefore, the church offered eternal hope for those **guilty** of venial sins, but not for mortal sins.

3.   The Reformers and the Concept of Sin

Martin Luther did away with the system of penance for Protestants, primarily because of the abuses he witnessed with the practice. Macquarrie wrote that penance was developed to take care of sins committed after baptism. The penitent was to make sincere confession of their sins, declare their genuine sorrow and their purpose of amending their

---

19   Carl F.H. Henry, *Baker's Dictionary of Christian Ethics*, (Grand Rapids: Baker Books, 1973),162.

20   Henry Thiessen, *Lectures in Systematic Theology.* (Grand Rapids: Eerdmans, 1979), 339.

life, and make restitution to those whom they had wronged.[21] The penance closely echoed the Hebraic sacrificial system where covenant people, after breaking the law, were required to confess their sin before a judge, express sorrow to the community, promise change and make restitution. After these conditions were met, the Israelite purchased a sacrifice, traveled to the temple, performed the sacrifice and came back to the judges, who made the community to understand full restitution was made. The problem was that Luther threw the baby out with the bathwater, resulting in Protestants today having a minimalist view of sin. I am under the conviction that Luther took away the value of sin, but Calvin took away the seriousness of sin for Protestants.

Feinberg argued that Calvin was best remembered for his eschatological and christological contribution to theology. In opposition to the Anabaptists, who emphasized the differences between the testaments, Calvin posited one covenant age of grace with different administrations, which he called dispensations. Central to his unity of the covenants was the covenant motif that stated the continuity between the Old and New was centered about John the Baptist. Thus Reformed Theology is an expression of a continuity system.[22] Calvin rejected all things that were portrayed as

---

21   John Macquarrie, *Dictionary of Christian Ethics*. (Philadelphia: Westminster Press, 1967). 249.

22   John S Feinberg, *Continuity and Discontinuity*. (Westchester, Illinois: Crossway Books, 1988), 38.

sin, even if not found in scripture, whereas the Anabaptists only rejected those things specifically portrayed as sin; that is why Anabaptists, Amish and Puritans had no problem with smoking and growing tobacco.

According to Bromiley, Calvin's most important contribution to the understanding of justification was his uniting of two things, which for purposes of clarity had in sense been divided, namely justification and sanctification. He believed that Christ justifies no one whom he does not at the same time sanctify.[23] This was important in understanding how he considered the concept of sin. Rather than the new birth just forgiving sin, leaving the new believer to seek holiness as needed, it now enabled the new believer to be holy immediately and immediately had the power to overcome the temptation of sin. For Calvin, once a believer was saved, there was no possibility of losing their salvation, and if you cannot be unsaved, sin takes on insignificance. However, there were other Reformers such as Johannes Wollebius (1586-1629) who taught on reprobation, the denial of unmerited grace once freely given.[24] Reprobates were not just those who rejected the gospel; but also included those who turned away from the gospel.

---

23   Geoffrey W. Bromiley, *Historical Theology: An Introduction.* (Grand Rapids: Eerdmans, 1978), 237.

24   Geoffrey W. Bromiley, *Historical Theology: An Introduction.* (Grand Rapids: Eerdmans, 1978), 331.

Feinberg believed the tendency to stress the historical and literal sense of a text against allegorism was stronger among the Reformed than among the Lutherans. For the Reformed, the moral laws and precepts of the OT were given added weight as guides to the Christian life.[25] The problem that arises is that if scripture is a mere guide, then sin becomes situational.

The Arminians presented a detailed position on apostasy in their "Sentenia Remonstrantium" to the Synod of Dort; that people do apostatizes. The most cited passage for their argument was Hebrews 6:4-6 from which they formulate that it was possible to apostatize, given the historical biblical record.[26] This was understandable after thousands of Anabaptists were murdered by Catholics, Calvinists and Lutherans for being re-baptized by immersion. The Schleitheim Confession in 1527 by the Anabaptists in Schleitheim, Switzerland demanded believers be separated from the evil and wickedness of the devil. They were not to fellowship with the wicked or participate in their abominations.[27] In a similar fashion, Menno Simons in his book, "On the Ban" (1550), defined church discipline for Anabaptist

---

25   John S Feinberg, *Continuity and Discontinuity*. (Westchester, Illinois: Crossway Books, 1988), 27.

26   Millard Erickson, *Christian Theology*. (Grand Rapids: Baker Books, 1983), 1002.

27   Hans Hillerbrand, *The Reformation*. (Grand Rapids: Baker Books, 1972), 235.

congregations: "Believers who do not remain obedient are **guilty** of rebellion and must be shunned and avoided by the congregation." Those banned were those who rejected church judgment, who lived in open sin, who were disorderly or who caused divisions.[28] The ban forever separated one-time members from their community; and so their concept of sin included actions that disrupted the community.

The Reformation cannot be considered without reference to the Catholic Church, which in June 1520 issued a papal bull, "Exsurge Domine". This document lists the 41 errors of Martin Luther. It claimed that mortal sins remain, that Purgatory is a real place and that the church has the power to excommunicate.[29] In a time when many Protestants considered the Pope as led by the devil, and cartoons depicted former Popes in hell, it was of little surprise that William Ames (1576-1633) argued that one can be in covenant with the devil as well as with God. Ames believed that it came about when faith and hope were transferred from God to the enemy by means of witchcraft or satanic compacts.[30] Though the Reformation would close with a broad spectrum of what believers considered sin, it would close with the birth

---

28   Ibid, Bromiley, 159.

29   Hans Hillerbrand, *The Reformation*. (Grand Rapids: Baker Books, 1972), 80.

30   Geoffrey W. Bromiley, *Historical Theology: An Introduction*. (Grand Rapids: Eerdmans), 307.

of the Age of Enlightenment. The modern church age would see a rise of humanistic beliefs that not only challenged every concept of sin, but syncretism with some of those beliefs brought a pollution of ideologies into the church.

4.   The Modern Church and the Concept of Sin

One of the most famous sermons ever written about the consequences of sin was by Jonathan Edwards in 1734, at Northampton, Massachusetts, called "A Sinner in the Hands of an Angry God." The sermon was based on Hebrews 10:31: "It is a terrifying thing to fall into the hands of the living God." Though the sermon was instrumental in birthing the Great Awakening, church history has proven that few are ever shamed into the kingdom, or come into the kingdom, because of the fear of hellfire.

Pope Pious IX (1846 – 1878) presided over the First Vatican Council, which decreed the dogma of papal infallibility. This pope also introduced, in 1854, the dogma of the Immaculate Conception of the Blessed Virgin Mary, which holds that Mary was pure of all sin including original sin. In response to the radical beliefs of the Age of Enlightenment, the pope also issued "Syllabus Errorum", which condemned Liberalism, Socialism and Rationalism. He believed these movements had a fundamental difference regarding the concept of sin.

Packer wrote how that in 1910, The General Assembly of the Northern Presbyterian Church specified five fundamentals of faith for evangelical Christianity. These include the inspiration and infallibility of scripture, the Deity of Christ, the virgin birth and miracles, the penal death of Christ for our sins and Christ's physical resurrection and return. These five articles became the doctrinal platform for later fundamentalist organizations.[31] In 1929, a set of 12 volumes called "The Fundamentals" were sent to every church in America; which included polemics against Romanism, Darwinism, Christian Science, Mormonism, Spiritualism and Jehovah Witnesses.[32] Far more than a disagreement of the deity of Christ, the fundamentalists had a different concept of sin. Dispensationalism had burst onto the church stage, in about the year 1900, with the view that all history could be cut up into periods of time, or dispensations. Feinberg argued the Abrahamic and Davidic covenants were generally viewed as unconditional covenants by Dispensationalists, but as conditional covenants by non-dispensationalists. Non-dispensationalists point out that the covenant promises are addressed to biological Jews for spiritual, social, political and economic blessings. The more one emphasizes the spiritual aspect alone, the more one's system stresses

---

31   J.J. Packer, *Fundamentalism and the Word of God.* (Grand Rapids: Eerdmans Publishing, 1958), 29.

32   Ibid, Packer, 28.

continuity. The more one emphasizes all four aspects of blessings, the more one's system stresses discontinuity.[33] Therefore, sin was fully defined as an aspect of a forfeiture of blessing within the covenant.

Feinberg also stated that the stress on discontinuity between the Law of Moses and the Law of Christ by Paul did not eliminate continuity either. Though the Christian was no longer bound to the Mosaic Law, the Christian was bound to Christ's law because some of the individual commandments remain authoritative as integrated into the law of Christ.[34] That simply meant that Christians were bound to a higher law that defined sin for Christians, just as the Mosaic Law had defined sin for the Israelites.

In 1927, at age 21, Bonhoeffer wrote his first dissertation, "The Communion of Saints", where he argued that the church of Christ, existing as community, is neither an ideal society with no need of reform or is it a gathering of the elite. Rather, it was a communion of sinners capable of being untrue to the gospel.[35] Bonhoeffer saw the church as a community of people who failed by sin. Without question, many churches today have lowered their ethical standards

---

33   John S Feinberg, *Continuity and Discontinuity*, (Westchester, Illinois: Crossway Books, 1988), 71.

34   Ibid, Feinberg, 217.

35   Geoffrey Kelly, "The Life and Death of a Modern Martyr", *Christianity Today*, (Issue 32, Vol. 10, No. 4), 9.

in order to bring in more people, to the point that some denominations have struggled with the ethical question of allowing homosexual ministers to remain in the ministry. Divorce today is as rampant among people who regularly attend church as those who only show up for funerals and weddings. Scott Rae argues that today, even among Christian couples contemplating marriage, abstinence until marriage is considered somewhat outdated, and it can no longer be assumed that committed Christian couples are not sexually active.[36] Churches that preach against sin are disappearing. There is a trend to have "Celebration services", which are a thinly masked, feel-good gospel where sin is never mentioned. Today, for many Christians, the Ten Commandments have become little more than the Ten Suggestions. Today, many Christians do not understand the seriousness of breaking covenants; whether they are covenants of marriage, covenants of church fellowship or financial covenants, such as credit cards and mortgages. Yet Jesus taught that every wrongdoing would receive just punishment (Mt 25:31-46), even for believers.

Braun raises the issue of divorce, with respect, not only to local church leadership but by missions also.[37] Though

---

36   Scott Rae, *Moral Choices*. (Grand Rapids: Zondervan Publishing, 1995), 25.

37   Michael Braun, *Second Class Christians*. (Dowers Grove, Illinois: InterVarsity Press, 1989), 89.

the traditional concept of missionaries who went to foreign fields to preach the gospel and teach people to flee from sin is long gone, today, Mission boards have evolved primarily into charitable organizations. Many mission boards require the expertise of specialized people, such as pilots and aeronautical mechanics, to get missionaries into remote areas. In addition, they need tradespeople to build and maintain buildings in the field. Lastly, they need professionals, such as doctors and teachers, to provide badly needed medical services and teaching. When these missions boards refuse people because they were once divorced, they severely curtail the list of available talented people. To find people, they lower ethical standards by redefining for their organization what sins are acceptable and which are not.

Theologians have divided the church age into many historical segments, according to church movements. As I have shown, the concept of sin has been continually changed to reflect the struggles each movement faced. Today, all denominations are under increasing pressure to change, and sadly for some churches that means lowering ethical standards. Church movements have been **guilty** of defining sin according to situational ethics rather than a biblical standard. It is my conviction that a new perspective on sin will impact how churches will consider their concept of sin.

Chapter 4

THE NEED FOR ORIGINAL LANGUAGE STUDY

I t was St. Augustine who confessed that a Christian leader who is to expound the scriptures must know Greek and Hebrew, in addition to Latin, otherwise it is impossible to avoid constant stumbling. There is a vast difference between a simple preacher and a person who expounds the scripture, for a simple preacher, even with biblical study helps, is unequal to the task of interpreting scripture.[38] In Luther's 1524 treatise, "To the Councilmen of all Cities in Germany That They Establish and Maintain Christian Schools", he wrote:

> "The languages are a sheath in which the sword of the Spirit is contained; they are the casket in which the jewel is enshrined; they are the vessel in which this wine is held; they are the larder in which the food is stored; and as the gospel itself

---

38   Gary Pratico, and Miles Van Pelt, *Basics of Biblical Hebrew Grammar.* (Grand Rapids: Zondervan, 2001), 119.

points out, they are the baskets in which are kept the loaves and fishes. If through our neglect we let the languages go, we shall lose the gospel."

Sadly, the prediction of Luther has come to pass in much of the Church today, because so few ministers have training in the original languages. Turn on the television on Sunday mornings and you will hear numerous preachers preach from the KJV, declaring it is the infallible word of God. It simply is not. The only infallible word of God are the original Hebrew and Greek scriptures. Erickson stated that the doctrine of inerrancy applies in the strict sense only to the originals, but in a derivative sense to copies and trans-lations, that is, to the extent that they reflect the original.[39] Considering the extraordinary circumstances when the KJV was interpreted, it was a considerable achievement, but remains flawed.

A.   The Problem with Translations

Though this study will reference the KJV, I will not try to find another version that uses a word that better suits my argument. I consider that to challenge the word translation of the KJV is a serious matter. Considering that the KJV was translated in the early 1600s, without the use of mod-ern-day computers, it was a marvelous achievement and

---

39   Millard Erickson, *Christian Theology*. (Grand Rapids: Baker Books, 1998), 265.

those men are to be commended. However, the purity of the Hebrew and Greek languages was lost. In 1603, when James ascended the throne, the Church of England was well established, but two other groups began to gain influence. The first group, the Puritans, wanted to "purify" the clergy and, therefore, opposed the bishops of the Church of England. The second group, called "Independents", included Calvinists and Baptists.[40] The Puritans had filled the House of Commons and used their newly acquired power to influence the translation of an English translation of the Bible. Therefore, the King James translation had significant political and moral motives, for they wanted a translation that did not support Catholicism or even Anglicanism, but also supported high moral values. Though Jerome in the 3rd century had translated the Hebrew and Greek texts into Latin (vulgate), and Martin Luther had translated the Bible into German in the 1640s, yet in 1611, rabbis and Eastern Orthodox clergy were never consulted for help. Jews had been banished in much of Europe and though not banished in England, they were despised. Added to this, the rift between the Puritans and the Catholics further separated access to the Greek Orthodox Church, who had maintained the Greek language. This left the Puritans with only two sources, the Latin and German translations. Even nature

---

40   Justo Gonzalez, *The Story of Christianity*, Vol. 2, *The Reformation to the Present Day*. (New York: Harper Publishers, 1985), 151.

teaches us that the further someone is from the source of a river, the greater the contamination of its water.

A simple example is the English word "Sabbath", which comes from the Hebrew word "shavat". However, the Greek word is "sabbaton". Not anxious to call it "sabbat", because that would be the Greek equivalent and a continual reminder of Catholicism, the Puritans chose the Hebrew equivalent. However, the problem was that the Puritans were not proficient in Hebrew and were not willing to ask the Jews as how to pronounce the word. They did not understand that Hebrew letters contained dots, some dots above or below represented a vowel, a dot in the middle of the letter either doubles the letter or changes it from a hard sound to a soft sound, and a dot above some letters added an "h" to soften the letter. For the letter "S", they chose a "s" sound like "set" instead of a "sh" sound, like in "ship". For the letter "B", they chose a "b" like "boy" instead of "v" sound, like in "love". For the letter "T", they chose a "th" like "there" instead of a "t" sound like "toy". Though they only had three letters to work with, they got all three wrong. That is why Christians pronounce "Sabbath" as "saab-bath", whereas the Jews continue to pronounce is as "shaa-vat".

The fact that the English word "Sabbath" is a poor translation of the original Hebrew word is of little consequence; but it is an example of what happens when theologians do not have original language skills. The following are several examples to prove that the translators of the KJV translation were **guilty** of faulty translation.

1.   Our Heavenly Mansions

Ask any Christian, and they will tell you that someday they will get a mansion in heaven. Not only did Jesus proclaim that there were many mansions in heaven for his followers, but hundreds of songs have been written about the joy one day when we all get to heaven and we all receive a mansion.

However, this raises a problem. Almost all of the parables revolve around the theme of reward. If the Lord will reward us, does that mean that some will receive mansions and some not? If there was no reward system, then we would all receive the same mansion without partiality, yet that is not substantiated in scripture. Jesus says there are many mansions, he does not say all are mansions! Is Jesus our heavenly Santa, giving out good presents to all? Or, does God have so much gold, silver and jewels that he uses them as common building products for our heavenly houses?

Context is critical in determining the meaning of a passage. John chapter 14 occurs after the last Passover, where Jesus encourages his disciples to love one another and tells Peter that he will deny him three times. After the first three verses of chapter 14, where the promise of mansions is given, Jesus continues with encouraging the disciples for what is about to happen. The surrounding context is of little help in determining what Jesus means by a "mansion", and the other Gospels are silent regarding the promise. To answer the question of "Do we all receive a mansion in Heaven?", let's look at the words of Jesus:

> "Let not your heart be troubled: ye believe in God, believe also in me. In my Father's house are many mansions: if it were not so, I would have told you. I go to prepare a place for you. And if I go and prepare a place for you, I will come again, and receive you unto myself; that where I am, there ye may be also" (Jn. 14:1-3).

Verse 2 begins with "in my Father's house", the word for "house" is "oikia" and means "dwelling, house, building or household".[41] The word is found 93 times in the NT and almost always refers to someone's home. Though Jesus called the temple, "my father's house" (Jn. 2:16), and though the word is used figuratively of our bodies as our earthly house (2 Cor. 5:1), nevertheless there is nothing to suggest it meant anything else than a place where a family lived. Verse 2 continues with "are many mansions". The Greek word for "many" is "pollai" and means "a very

---

41   Frederick Danker, A Greek-English Lexicon of the New Testament. (Chicago: University of Chicago Press, 2000), 695.

large number".[42] It was a common adjective to describe a large quantity of items. The Greek word for mansions is "monai", which means "a dwelling place, room or state of remaining in an area, staying."[43] Verse 2 concludes with the phrase "prepare a place for you," which is composed of the words "etoimaso topon". The word "etoimaso" is a verb that means, "I will prepare," or "I will make ready."[44] The word "topon" means "a place of habitation, an area, a region."[45] Therefore, this phrase could be literally translated, "In my father's house many stay, if it were not so, I would have told you. I go to prepare a place of habitation for you." The word "topon" is found 94 times in the NT scripture and comes into the English language as the root for the English word "topography". It is used in the Gospels of the dry places where the unclean spirit walks (Mt 12:43), a desert place Jesus went to pray (Mt 14:13), famines, pestilences and earthquakes will occur in many places (Mt 24:7), Daniel stood in the holy place (Mt 24:15), the place where the body of Jesus lay (Mt 28:6), the place where Jesus fed the 5,000 (Mk 6:35), the place of the skull (Mk 14:22), the place in the

---

42   Frederick Danker, A Greek-English Lexicon of the New Testament. (Chicago: University of Chicago Press, 2000), 847.

43   Ibid, Danker, 658.

44   Ibid, Danker, 401.

45   Ibid, Danker, 1011.

Book of Isaiah that Jesus read (Lk 4:17), the places Jesus sends the seventy (Lk 10:1), the lowest place in a banquet room (Lk 14:9), the place of torment (Lk 16:28), a place in the garden of Olives (Lk 22:40), the Pool of Bethesda was the place where the infirmed man was healed (Jn 5:13) and the place where John baptized (Jn 10:40). Though Paul uses the word figuratively, "do not give place to the devil," the word "topon" is a generic word that does not indicate a mansion, but rather a locality.

The Apostle Peter speaks of our eternal reward; "an inheritance incorruptible, and undefiled, and that fades not away, reserved in heaven for you" (1 Pet. 1:4). This may have prompted the Puritans, who translated the King James Version, to use literary license to insert the word "mansion". Certainly God would not be cheap, his very nature tells us that he is a generous God who owns all the gold and silver; so it is perfectly natural that when he builds a home for his children, that the homes would be far better than a man-made house, and the only word that clearly describes the best home man can make is "mansion". I live in a modern city where there are wealthy communities with million-dollar homes, but my city also has older communities with run-down houses, mobile home parks and government subsi-dized housing projects.

Though God may make glorious homes for us in heaven, that does not mean we all get a mansion; because it would mean we all receive the same reward. It makes little sense that the thief on the cross would receive the same eternal rewards as a man or woman of God who has dedicated their life, even sacrificially, for the proclamation of the Gospel. Most of the Lord's parables about heaven speak of servant-hood. In servant-hood, a servant serves someone above them. If the heavenly rewards include rulership over cities, it is not just us serving Jesus, but many serving the ruler placed by Jesus to rule. This creates a hierarchy of rule, meaning some are elevated to high positions and others are lowered to low positions. If the size of a dwelling is commiserate to the office, then some dwellings will be far more splendid than others.

In conclusion, I have no difficulty believing our eternal place will be glorious, and many will receive a glorious home, but there is little theological ground to argue that we all get a mansion. It is easy to understand that the Puritans believed that a place of habitation built by God would be magnificent, far better than human hands could build, and therefore it is easy to understand how they came to the conclusion of using the word "mansion". However, it implies something that is not in the text; the idea of everyone getting a mansion. Therefore, they were **guilty** of adding to scripture an idea not supported by the original language.

2.   Joseph's Coat of Many Colors

Ask any Christian, and they will tell you that Jacob gave his son, Joseph, a coat of many colors, because that it what the KJV records. "Israel loved Joseph more than all his children, because he was the son of his old age, and he made him a coat of many colors" (Gen. 37:3). The problem arises when, in Hebrew, the words for "many" and "colors" do not exist in this verse. Rather, a word describing not the color but the shape of the garment was used. The Hebrew word translated as "a coat" correctly means "a tunic".[46] This was an outer garment, similar to the garments worn by Arabs today. The Hebrew word translated as "many" correctly means "flat of hands" [47] and the word translated as "colors" correctly means "bottom of feet", indicating the length of the garment, "a long flowing tunic that was long-sleeved and flowed to the floor." The word for "many" in Hebrew is "rabbiym", which is not found in this verse. The word for "color" in Hebrew is "chatub" and also is not found in the verse.[48] Another word, "takelet", refers to violet cloth worn by priests and kings, which also in not found in the verse.[49] If the verse does have these words, why would "long-sleeved, floor-length" be replaced with "many colors"? There are

---

46   F. Brown, S. Driver, and C. Briggs, *The Brown-Driver-Briggs Hebrew and English Lexicon*, (Peabody, Mass.: Hendrickson, 2003), 509.

47   Ibid, BDB, 821.

48   Ibid, BDB, 310.

49   F. Brown, S. Driver, and C. Briggs, *The Brown-Driver-Briggs Hebrew and English Lexicon*, (Peabody, Mass.: Hendrickson, 2003), 1067.

three words for something that could be described as a coat; the ephod, the robe and the tunic. All three are used to describe the garments of the High Priest. "And these are the garments that they shall make; a breastplate, and an ephod, and a robe and a broidered tunic, a mitre, and a girdle" (Ex 28:6).

The word for tunic is "kethoneth", and is found 29 times in scripture.[50] The first reference is the "coat" of skins God gave to Adam and Eve (Gen. 3:21). Job makes reference to his tunic (Job 30:18). The word is used to describe the robe of the high priest (Ex 28:4), it was made of fine linen (Ex 28:39) and was colored blue, purple, red and gold (Ex 39:29). All the other Levites also had coats, or tunics (Ex 40:14). These tunics were worn next to the skin. Tamar, the king's daughter, wore a robe (or tunic) with many colors, indicating those that wore it were virgins (2 Sam. 13:18). Isaiah prophesies about how God will raise up Eliakim after the destruction of Jerusalem, a ruler who will wear a tunic, a father of Judah, the government will be upon his shoulders and a man in the lineage of Christ (Isa. 22:21). Ezra speaks of the 100 priests tunics that were made when the children of Israel returned to Jerusalem after the captivity (Ezr 2:70). The remnant that return under Nehemiah bring 530 priests garments (tunics) back to Jerusalem (Neh 7:70). Note that the purpose of these garments is to indicate authority.

---

50   Ibid, BDB, 509.

Adam and Eve had authority as the first man and woman. The priests have authority in the temple. A member of the royal family has authority, even if they were yet but a young virgin. Rulers had legislative authority. Their authority was identified by their tunic. Gaglardi argued that that tunic represented salvation, because it covered the whole body like salvation.[51] However, ancient society would not have seen it as a symbol of salvation, but as a symbol of authority.

Another word for garment is the "ephod", which the boy Samuel wore (2 Sam. 2:18). This is the same word used to describe the ephod, one of six pieces of clothing, which were worn by the High Priest (Ex 25:7). This garment had several colors and had stones on each shoulder (Ex 28:6,9). Gideon made an ephod out of the garment and jewelry he confiscated from the kings of Midian (Judg. 8:27). Micah made an ephod for his son, who he made a priest in his house of idols (Judg. 17:5). King Saul slew 85 priests who wore ephods (1 Sam. 22:18). When David's family was taken captive, he had Abithar, the priest, bring an ephod, which he used as a contact to ask the Lord if he should go to war (1 Sam. 30:7). Hosea prophesied that Israel, for many days, will have no king, no sacrifice, no ephod and no teraphim (Hos. 3:4). David brought up the ark from the house of Obed-edom, wearing both a outer robe of fine linen and an ephod (1 Chr. 15:27). Note that the purpose

---

51   Maureen Gaglardi, *The Path of the Just.* (Vancouver: New West Press, 1971), 59.

of an ephod is separateness, or an uniqueness, and every reference is linked to the priesthood.

The next word for garment is "bimiyl", which is usually translated as "robe", or "cloke", and is found in scripture 27 times; mostly in reference to the High Priest's garments.[52] One of the six pieces of clothing the high priest wore was the outer robe (Ex 28:4). Like the ephod, it was made of fine linen embroidered with threads of blue, violet, red and gold. David cut off a piece of King Saul's outer coat (1 Sam. 24:11). When Saul approached the witch at En-dor, he was wearing a mantle (2 Sam. 28:14). Isaiah describes the righteous as:

"For he put on righteousness as a breastplate, and a helmet of salvation upon his head, and he put on the garments of vengeance for clothing, and was clad with zeal as a cloke" (Isa. 59:17).

Isaiah repeats this, "for he has clothed me with the garments of salvation, he has covered me with a robe of righteousness" (Isa. 61:10). The psalmist cried, "let my adversaries be clothed with shame like a mantle" (Ps 109:29). The purpose of a "robe" is covering.

The last word to represent a garment is "mantle". The best-known mantle is Elijah's, who took up the mantle of

---

52   F. Brown, S. Driver, and C. Briggs, The Brown-Driver-Briggs
        Hebrew and English Lexicon, (Peabody, Mass.: Hendrickson,
        2003), 591.

Elijah when it fell from him (2 Kgs 2:13). This is the same word that is used of the Babylonian garment that Achan hid (Josh. 7:21). When Jonah preached to Ninevah, all the people including the king repented. The king of Ninevah arose from his throne, laid his robe down, covered himself with sackcloth and sat in ashes (Jon. 3:6). His robe, or mantle, signified his authority.

Zechariah prophesied that "it shall come to pass in that day that the prophets shall be ashamed and neither shall they wear a rough garment of hair" (Zec 13:4). Only worn by kings and prophets, the mantle represented unlimited authority.

To try and figure why the Puritans chose these words during the translation of the King James Version is speculative and would accomplish little. Generally, a coat is made to keep a person warm, and that would make sense in cold English winters. It is apparent that the Puritans identified Joseph's coat to be like the multi-colored, high priest garments. We can chalk it up to literary license, but it would be irresponsible to continue the idea among theologians. Changing Sunday School stories, however, would probably prove futile. Theologically, one would have to argue that since the same word is used for the garments from animal, that God made Adam and Eve, that those garments were also of many colors. The biblical use of the word "tunic" can be determined by use in scripture as a long-sleeved, flowing-to-the-floor garment that was made of a variety of materials, animal skins, fine linen and coarser linen. The tunic was worn to portray authority, the ephod was worn to represent separateness and the outer robe was worn as a covering, and a mantle represented unlimited authority. Barbara Bowen states that only two people in each clan were privileged to wear the garment, the sheikh and his appointed heir. It often was a white garment worn under an outer coat, because in the heat when the coat is removed, the garment still identified the clan leader.[53] There is a well-known photo of President George Bush walking alongside the king of Saudi Arabia, who is dressed in a traditional, centuries-old, long-flowing, single-colored Arabic garment. I believe the garment given by Jacob to Joseph was very similar.

It is apparent that the idea of his robe having many colors sprang from the many colors of the high priest garments, but this addition has no scriptural foundation. When theologians are **guilty** of being ignorant of ancient cultures, they impose their own reasoning, and the result is flawed theology.

3.   The Love of Money

Most people are familiar with the biblical phrase, "the love of money is the root of all evil" (1 Tim. 6:10). However,

---

53   Barbara Bowen, *Strange Scriptures that Perplex the Western Mind.* (Grand Rapids: Eerdmans, 1987), 43.

to fully understand this verse, it is imperative to consider the original Greek words for "love".

The Greeks had 4 words for love. To express love toward their gods, they used the word "agape".[54] To express love to a brother or sister, they used the word "phileo", as found in the name "Philadelphia" (city of brotherly love). The name Philemon means "Affectionate One".[55] To express their love towards a woman, they called sexual love, or "eros", from which we get the term "erotic". There are no biblical references for this word. Lastly, the Greeks called family love "stergo". Again, there are no biblical references. Notice that every object of love is a god or a person. Today, we often say we love our car, we love our home, we love our cellphone or we love our goldfish. The Greeks could not imagine loving a common object, such as a house or mere possessions. Perhaps they were wiser than us. The phrase "love of money" is only found in 1 Timothy.

> "But they that will be rich fall into temptation and a snare, and into many foolish and hurtful lusts, which drown men in destruction and perdition. For the love of money is the root of all evil: which while some coveted after, they have erred from the faith, and pierced themselves through with many sorrows. But thou, O man of God, flee these things;

---

54   Frederick Danker, *A Greek – English Lexicon*. (Chicago: University of Chicago Press, 2000), 1056.

55   Ibid, Danker, 6.

and follow after righteousness, godliness, faith, love, patience, meekness" (1 Tim. 6:9-11).

Here Paul is instructing Timothy to flee from coveting money, for those who covet money will experience sorrow in life; but he, rather, is to seek after doing right, living godly, having faith, patience and meekness. Society in Paul's time functioned much like society today, those with money enjoyed a better life and, therefore, people yearned to be financially independent. The problem is that some become wealthy at the expense of others, and it is the treatment of others that becomes a snare. If the "love" of money is the problem, what "love" was Paul referring to?

The phrase "the love of money is the root of all evil" in Greek is "philarguria riza gar panton ka-kon estin." The Greek word "philarguria" means "the avaricious, or the miserly".[56] Therefore, the word for "love" in this biblical quotation is not the word "love" at all but the word "philarguria", which means "avarice or miserliness regarding money". Webster defines the word avarice to mean "greed for money", and the word "miserliness" to mean a person who lives in discomfort or squalor in order to hoard his wealth. Like our society today, the Greeks understood that for society to function, there must be a liberal trade of goods

56   Frederick Danker, *A Greek – English Lexicon.* (Chicago: University of Chicago Press, 2000), 1056.

and services accomplished by the exchange of finances. The person who hoards disrupts the system.

The Greek word for "root" is "riza", which is a noun that was used to describe the portion of plant life beneath the surface of the soil.[57] The Greek word "gar" is a preposition that means "for". The word "panton" is an adjective that means "all", which implies no exclusion. The word "kakon" is an adjective that means "the state of wickedness, depravity, or vice that comes from a mean spirited person."[58] Danker argues that this word also comes from the root word "kakos", as a noun that means "evil, bad, morally reprehensible". Therefore, this word means "of the bad, of the evil or of the wicked." The word "estin" is an adjective that simply means "to be" or "is". When these five words are put together, it reads, "root" + "for" + "all" + "of the evil", or in better English, "the root of all evil is."

Paul's quotation continues with a warning of those who are greedy, they become "apeplanethesan", which means "they were led astray."[59] In context, it is indicative of a simple past action that was received by the subject; thus it implies, "they have erred from the faith piercing themselves with great mental anguish." Their miserliness was a product

---

57   Ibid, Danker, 905.

58   Ibid, Danker, 500.

59   Ibid, Danker, 119.

of being taken advantage by someone in the past and, to protect themselves, they hoard.

This verse tells us the source of all viciousness toward others is the miserly, greedy person who lives in squalor, but hoards money, because they were led astray from the faith by former events, resulting in themselves being pierced by great mental and spiritual anguish. We are all **guilty** at some time of having a hidden agenda of getting ahead, of making money a priority in life. It appears to be a linear scale, the greater the priority to get money, the greater the consequences of having money.

Love is usually an emotion that expresses the purest of affection toward another person, but here the Puritans use it in a negative context to express the fullest affection toward something evil. The problem arises is that it supports the Arian theory that spirit is good and matter is bad. You are not more spiritual because you are poor.

4.   You are Gods

There is a psalm where the KJV declares that God judges among the gods and that his children are gods:

> "A Psalm of Asaph. God stands in the congregation of the mighty; he judges among the gods ... I have said, you are gods and all of you are children of the most High" (Ps 82:1,6).

This is a curious verse, but other translations merely say he judges among the mighty. In the Hebrew, verse 1 consists of only 8 words. The first word is "mizmor", which means "melody or psalm", as from a song.[60] This is a verb that means "to make music" and is found in the titles of 57 psalms. The second word is "le-asaph", which means "in regard to those gathered."[61] The word "asaph" is a noun that means "gatherer".[62] Translated into English, it is "Asaph", the name of a man who gathered writings, such as Psalms, together. Adding the first two words, we arrive at "A psalm to the gatherer". The third word is "Elohim", the name of Creator God. The name of God here acts as a descriptor of the gatherer, so adding the third word, we arrive at, "A psalm to the gatherer, Elohim". The fourth word is "nitsab", which means, "to take one's stand," or "be positioned like a watchman."[63] This verb is a simple passive action, there-fore it is correctly translated as "he was standing" or "he stood". Adding this word to the phrase, we now arrive at, "A psalm to the gatherer, Elohim, he stood". The fifth word is

---

60   F. Brown, S. Driver, C. Briggs, *The Brown-Driver-Briggs Hebrew and English Lexicon*. (Peabody, Mass.: Hendrickson, 2003), 274.

61   Ibid, BDB, 510.

62   Ibid, BDB, 62.

63   F. Brown, S. Driver, C. Briggs, *The Brown-Driver-Briggs Hebrew and English Lexicon*. (Peabody, Mass.: Hendrickson, 2003), 662.

"ba'adat-el", which is a word that consists of the root word "adat", which means "congregation". The suffix "el" means "god", "angel", "mighty one".[64] The word "el" is singular, therefore "gods" would not work. In addition, it is connected to the first word with a "maqqef", the small horizontal line, therefore this construction literally means "in a mighty congregation". This dismisses the translation of "gods". Adding this word to the phrase, we now arrive at, "A psalm to the gatherer, Elohim, he stood in a mighty congregation". The sixth word is "be'qereb", which has a root word "qereb" that means "among, in the midst, from among or inward part."[65] As a verb, it means "to come near".[66] Adding this word to the phrase, we now arrive at, "A psalm to the gatherer, Elohim, he stood with a mighty congregation in its midst". The seventh word is "Elohim", the Creator God. Adding this word to the phrase, we now arrive at, "A psalm to the gatherer, Elohim, he stood with a mighty congregation in its midst, Elohim". The last word is "yi'shepit", which is a verb that means "to judge",[67] but with incomplete action. Thus, it literally means that the subject doing the action, in this case judging, has begun to judge but has not finished, therefore "he judges." Adding this word to the phrase, we now arrive at, "A psalm

---

64   Ibid, BDB, 417.

65   Ibid, BDB, 899.

66   Ibid, BDB, 897.

67   Ibid, BDB, 1047.

to the gatherer, Elohim, he stood with a mighty congregation in its midst, Elohim judges." This phrase is somewhat difficult to understand in English, but understanding that the Hebrew language is almost totally void of punctuation, a better translation using English punctuation would be: "A psalm to the gatherer, Elohim: he stood with a mighty congregation; in its midst, Elohim judges."

Psalm 82:1 is relatively short and, after describing Elohim as the one who judges in the midst of the congregation in heavenly places, the psalmist immediately compares Elohim to the judges on earth, who utterly fail to judge righteously.

Verse 6 reads, "I have said, you are gods and all of you are children of the most High". Once again, this verse is problematic. The first Hebrew word is "aniy-omart", which consists of two parts. The first part means "I".[68] The second part is the root word "omart", which is a verb that means "to say".[69] The second word is "Elohim". Adding the first two words together, it means, "I, Elohim, say". The third word "atem" is a pronoun that means "you", referencing not a single person but a group. Adding the three words together, it means, "I, Elohim, say unto you". The fourth word is "wu'ben'ey", which means "and my sons". Adding the four

---

68   F. Brown, S. Driver, C. Briggs, *The Brown-Driver-Briggs Hebrew and English Lexicon.* (Peabody, Mass.: Hendrickson, 2003), 58.

69   Ibid, BDB, 50.

words together, it means, "I, Elohim, say unto you and my sons". The fifth word is "Eliyon", which is a proper name and title of God.[70] This title specifically portrays his character as "The one who lifts up." Adding the five words together, it means, "I, Elohim, say unto you and my sons, the one who lifts up". The sixth word is "kul'kem", which means "all of them". Adding the six words together, it means, "I, Elohim, say unto you and my sons, the one who lifts up all of them." Better English might be, "I, the Lord say unto you and to my sons, I am the one who lifts all them up."

Therefore, the English translation is poor, but with a better translation we see how a psalm was written to glorify the gatherer, Elohim, who stands in the midst of a mighty congregation where he judges. The psalmist then compares Elohim to judges on earth, who utterly fail to judge righteously, but once again speaks of God's righteousness, the one who lifts all them up: those who suffer from the unrighteous judges. The psalmist then concludes the psalm by declaring God will come to judge the earth, unjust judges will perish and God will inherit all nations.

The problem with this verse, as interpreted by the Puritans, is that it conflicts with Isaiah's declaration of Yahweh, "Is there a God beside me? yea, there is no God; I know not any" (Isa. 44:8). The psalm will be later used by the Mormon Church, as the central verse they use to

---

70   Ibid, BDB, 751.

defend their belief that when Mormons die, they become "gods" equal to Jesus. There is a considerable difference between "God stands in the congregation of the mighty; he judges among the gods ... I have said, you are gods and all of you are children of the most High," and "A psalm to the gatherer, Elohim: he stood with a mighty congregation; in its midst Elohim judges ... I, the Lord say unto you and to my sons, I am the one who lifts all them up." Once again, the Puritans were **guilty** of a poor translation that opened the door to poor theology.

Chapter 5

THE PROBLEM WITH COMMENTARIES

I t has been well established that a translation from one language to another loses a measure of accuracy. I also recognize that this loss of accuracy has led to an inaccuracy by commentaries, biblical dictionaries and lexicons regarding the meaning of words. One of my seminary professors often said that commentaries are thought-stoppers, because people thought that if well-educated men of God had come to these conclusions, that they must be right and there is no need for themselves to study or question their conclusions. That is why Seminary professors stress to their students the importance of researching the text first and, as a backup, go to commentaries for support for their ideas and to ensure they are not entertaining heresy. The following are several biblical examples where commentaries have failed.

1. Joseph and Mary

Most Christmas plays portray the birth of Jesus to two young people, Joseph and Mary, who travel to Bethlehem only to find no room at the Inn. Because the Christmas story traditionally tells of Joseph and Mary, the shepherds and the wise men, there is a natural assumption that his brothers and sisters were born to Mary and Joseph after Jesus. However, there may be more tradition in this story than most of us would like to admit.

Years later, during his ministry in Nazareth, Jesus taught in the synagogue and the townsfolk, who were well acquainted with the family, were amazed at his knowledge of the Word of God. They asked:

"Is not this the carpenter, the son of Mary, the brother of James, and Joses, and of Juda, and Simon? and are not his sisters here with us"? (Mk 6:3).

Historical church documents help shed some light. Theophylact says: "Joseph, the husband of the blessed Mary, had seven children by a former wife, four sons and three daughters – Martha, Esther and Salome, whose son John was; therefore Salome was reckoned our Lord's sister, and John was his nephew." In a manuscript of the Greek Testament in the Imperial Library of Vienna, numbered 34 in Lambecius's catalogue, there is a marginal note, which agrees pretty much with the account given above by Theophylact:

> "John the evangelist was cousin to our Lord Jesus Christ according to the flesh; for Joseph, the spouse of the God-bearing virgin, had four sons by his own wife, James, Simon, Jude, and Joses; and three daughters, Esther, and Thamar, and a third who, with her mother, was called Salome, who was given by Joseph in marriage to Zebedee; of her, Zebedee begot James, and John also the evangelist."

The writer of the manuscript professes to have taken this account from the commentaries of St. Sophronius. This agrees with Mark 6:3, which lists four brothers, James, Joses, Juda and Simon, along with at least two sisters. There appears to be no reason that Theophylact, Lambecius or Sophronius would have anything to gain by fabrication of this detail of the family structure of Mary and Joseph. If the details are in fact correct, they would explain a number of questions about the history behind the gospels. In the ancient world, the absence of quality paper and the awkwardness of clay tablets meant that most people memorized stories that they then passed onto their children. The Gospel writers chose to write down on papyrus scrolls as a more permanent record (Lk 1:1) the eyewitness accounts of the life of Christ. The writers of the gospels were not historians but rather theologians, and so their references to historical figures was meant only as a framework of reference. John only chooses seven events, whereas the others chose many more, but together they comprise only a small account of the actual events. As writers, they chose only those stories that supported the theme and purpose of their gospel. For that reason, many of extraneous details are left out. If I were to tell you that I will be visiting my aunt and uncle in Toronto tomorrow, you automatically know the only way for me to get to Toronto is by an airline. I do not have to explain what an airplane, an airport or a pilot is. Nor do I have to explain my whole family line, as to the names of all my relatives. So the family structure of Joseph is missing, because it is not important in the portrayal of Christ as the Messiah.

The first question that the story of the birth of Jesus asks is why did Mary travel with Joseph from Nazareth to Bethlehem for the required census by Caesar Augustus? This contradicts Jewish marriage customs. If we use the parable of the wise and foolish virgins in Matthew 25 as a model for Jewish marriage, the engaged couple would not be able to live together and the espoused virgin, Mary, would not have been able to travel with Joseph. However, the Pharisees and Sadducees would have made an exception to the rule in the case of the death of a mother of small children. If Salome indeed had died, possibly in childbirth, there would have been either an infant or at least two or more toddlers that Joseph would have had to care for. Since there is a strong family structure in Judaism, the Pharisees would quite possibly have approved the arrangement for Mary to live with Joseph, with the condition of refraining from sexual intercourse with the provision that Mary take personal care of the children. If Joseph indeed had seven kids from possible 1 to 15 in age, he would desperately need someone to take care of his children.

This also answers the next question, why did Joseph, as recorded in Matthew 1:25, not have sex with Mary until after the birth of Jesus? The account of the angel who spoke to Joseph does not mention a restriction of no sex; only that Joseph was to take Mary as his wife, which would give him full permission. A young Joseph would, like any young man, would have exercised his marital rights, but an older Joseph, having 7 kids, would have been much more willing to waver his rights, especially in view that he was still possibly in sorrow with the passing of his first wife. The Protoevangelium of James records the story of Mary, who raised in the temple of Jerusalem and at age 16 was espoused to Joseph in order to care for his children. Though this document may well be dismissed as questionable by many, it provides a real possibility of a young woman espoused to an older man.

The third question raised concerns the manger. We know the Hasmodian rule created three religious parties; the Sadducees, the Pharisees and the Essenes. The

Essenes were the religious party of the Samaritans. Each of them were required to have a trade and they all put their monies into a common pot, where they all benefited from the finances as a community. At about 5 PM each day, they stopped worked, came together, bathed, put on white robes, ate a meal and read the scriptures before returning home. They took oaths of charity. In the story of the Good Samaritan, the third man was an Essene who provided for the badly beaten man. The community of Essene priests in Quram did not marry and dedicated their lives as scribes; from this group, we have the Dead Sea Scrolls. When Jesus traveled from town to town, he and his disciples never had a problem with lodging because of the Essenes. Therefore, the presence of the Essenes in Bethlehem creates a problem with the lack of room in the Inn. The Essenes would have had a network that easily could have provided a room in someone's house for a man and his pregnant wife. However, if the party was not of two, but of nine, it dramatically changes things. A party of nine could only be put in a crowded town in a shelter such as a barn.

The fourth question deals with the trip to Egypt. We know that Joseph was a carpenter, however, as a young man, possibly under 20, he would still be in an apprenticeship under an older tradesman. To take your family to a strange country would have been nearly impossible for a younger man. If Joseph had indeed seven children, this would make him at least his middle thirties, if not mid-forties. At his older age, he would have the confidence that he could find work in Egypt as a tradesman. Also, the trip would be less daunting to a more experienced man.

This leads to the fifth question, what happened to Joseph? At the time of the crucifixion, Mary would be about 45 and Joseph about 50, if it is assumed that they were both very young. This is a traditional belief, not based on scripture, but on the average marriage age of couples. Since this story has its foundation in the Puritan Movement, and as Puritans they believe in "Solo Scriptura", or nothing but the Bible, they would have imposed an early age on Mary and Joseph according to their own traditions. Mary indeed could have been in her teens or twenties; we simply have no evidence from the Gospels. However, an older man would now be about 65 to 70, and thus a natural death would mean that the authors of the gospels would not consider his passing as noteworthy.

With the passing of Joseph, Mary is now the matriarch of the family. The provision of the elderly was the responsibility of the eldest son. That is why the eldest son received a double portion of inheritance at the time of his father's death, if his father's wife was still alive; he used it to provide for his mother. There is no traditional evidence that the eldest son received a double portion if the father's wife was dead. If Mary had seven children after Jesus, at the death of the oldest son, the next eldest son automatically would have provided for her. Yet Jesus on the Cross made provision for Mary, declaring the disciple to be her son (Jn 19:26). This would have been unnecessary if Mary had other children after Jesus. Older children from a previous marriage would not have been lawfully obligated to provide for their stepmother.

Lastly, the last question deals with the Zealots. After the Hasmodian rule ended with the Romans putting Herod as King over Judea, the Zealot party arose in opposition. They were a band of assassins who raided Roman outposts in an attempt to remove Roman rule. Their mandate was to once again put a man on the throne who was of the royal line of David. One of the disciples of Jesus, Simon the Zealot (Lk 6:15), belonged to this group. Paul refers to the group in Acts 21:38 as assassins. Having a member in the core group around Jesus, the Zealots were able to monitor the movements and teachings of Jesus. The Zealots were well aware of the royal lineage of Jesus. If Jesus was the eldest son of Mary and Joseph, this party would have make a great effort to make him king. When the people tried to make Jesus king by force (Jn 6:15), it was because of his miracles, not because he was in direct line to the throne. Therefore, both the people and the Zealots did not argue with Pilate when he asked them what he is to do with the King of the Jews (Mk 15:12). In their minds, Jesus was not next in line as king because he was the 5th son of Joseph, thus he had no legitimate claim to the throne.

In conclusion, the fact that Mary only had one child or eight children means very little. It does not affect our doctrine of Christology or of the Trinity. Many Evangelicals reject the idea that Mary had only one son, because they say that it reinforces the Catholic view of her "immaculate conception". I reject the idea that we must support an alternative non-catholic view, simply because we are obligated to believe differently. Nevertheless, it does cause us to reconsider how much of the Christmas story is tradition and how much is factual.

When I presented my research of Mary and Joseph to one of my seminary professors, he praised me for my research. The professor stated that though he agreed with the research, he was bound by church affiliation never to speak about it publicly. His ministerial accreditations required him to teach only one story, that Joseph and Mary were teenagers. He stated that Catholics believe in the Mary Immaculate, that is she, like Jesus, had no sin. Cyril of Alexandria, a fourth-century church bishop stated at the Council of Trent that Mary was "ever virgin".[71] Though the historical documents prove that Jesus was Mary's only son, Protestant leaders are not willing to acknowledge these documents because they open a can of worms. My argument is that truth always prevails. Unfortunately, Protestants are also **guilty** of having their sacred traditions.

---

71   Alister McGrath, *The Christian Theology Reader*. (Oxford, England: Blackwell Publishers 2000), 266.

2.   Did Jesus Own a House?

Jesus is often portrayed as a prophet that owned little in life, but that his Father in heaven daily provided for him. Christians sing songs like "I'm a Rich Poor Man" that has lyrics that proclaim, like Jesus, they are passing through this world with nothing, but they have wealth abundant in heaven.

In the Gospel Of Matthew, there are three references to "his own city", which all refer to Capernaum, his home base of his ministry in Galilee (Mt 4:13, 9:1, 11:23). According to Matthew, Jesus entered into a ship and passed over, and came into his own city (Mt 9:1). The Greek word for "his own or one's own" is "idios", which means "belonging to, having an exclusive relationship with," and was often used in reference to a person's home or possessions.[72] Therefore, the people in Capernaum would have been knowledgeable enough to point out to a stranger the street where Jesus lived. Matthew also wrote that Jesus left Nazareth and settled in Capernaum (Mt 4:13). The word "settled" is the Greek word "katokesen", which is a verb that means "he is living there or he is dwelling there."[73] It is a simple statement of a past or current action by the subject of the sentence, in this case Jesus. This word does not refer to a passing

---

72   Frederick Danker, *A Greek – English Lexicon.* (Chicago: University of Chicago Press, 2000), 466.

73   Ibid, Danker, 534.

or temporary stay, but a place where people establish their business and settle, raising a family. There is no concept of "renting a house" in the ancient world, even the stay in an Inn was temporary for travelers. This word would never be used for a traveler passing through a region, but was exclusively used for permanent citizens.

After coming into Capernaum, Jesus healed the paralytic and then called Matthew to follow him (Mt 9:9). This event is joined immediately with a second event where Jesus is reclining at the table in the house. "And it came to pass, as Jesus sat at meat" (Mt 9:10). This sentence in Greek is "kai egeneto autou anakeimenou en te oikia." The Greek word "kai" means "and", which joins the phrase to the previous verse. The next Greek word is "egeneto", which means "he brought it about, he made it happen or he performed it." Therefore, this verb means more than simply "it came to pass", but that the subject, "Jesus", was the principle agent in bringing the activity about. This phrase is followed by the word "autou", which means "he is the same man", thus it refers back to the subject "Jesus", a single male individual. The next Greek word is "anakeimenou", which means "reclining at a table",[74] that is, he was dining or had just finished a meal and was now in conversation with friends. If Jesus initiated this meal, and since there was a sufficient crowd of disciples, tax collectors and sinners with him; the

---

74   Ibid, Danker, 65.

cost of the meal would have been significant. Jesus would have to had to pay for the cost of the food and at least hire people to prepare the food, thus paying several people wages for preparing the food. The Greek word "en" means "in", and the word "te" means "the". The word "oikia" means "a house with property and possessions". Therefore, it was a physical building on a parcel of land clearly defined with boundaries, having furniture and possessions capable of making it a dwelling for a family as opposed to a dwelling place for animals. This root word is the same for the word "oikonomos", which is "steward", thus in context the subject, Jesus, was the steward of a house in Capernaum. In conclusion, the phrase could read, "And Jesus brought about a meal, and then reclined at the table in his own house."

If the house belonged to someone else, the scripture would have specifically noted who the house belonged to, such as Peter's house (Mt 8:5). Likewise, Matthew clearly states that Jesus was in a house that belonged to someone else, "And when Jesus came into the ruler's house" (Mt 9:23). Here, Matthew is careful to state a different house.

Matthew records the story of the tax collectors collecting taxes in the city of Capernaum from Peter and Jesus. The tax collectors were "they that received tribute money" (Mt 17:24). Here, the word "tribute" is the Greek word "didrachma", which was a double drachma or two coins each worth a drachma. A drachma was worth two days wages, so a didrachma was worth 4 days wages. It was paid annually to the temple by every Jewish male of age twenty or more, regardless of their wealth (rich or poor) at the time of census, for the maintenance of the temple (Ex 30:11-16). The tax collectors, in their census-taking of Capernaum, would not have approached Jesus and Peter if they did not own a house in Capernaum. Jesus and Peter are in Capernaum and after Peter is approached by the tax collectors, he enters the house where Jesus asks him if kings pay tribute (Mt 17:24). The phrase "and coming into the house" in context must be the home of Jesus. The tax collectors would have gone to Peter's house if they wanted Peter to pay his tax, but they went to the home of Jesus, not just to collect his tax, but may well have been trying to confirm rumors of Jesus's disloyalty to the temple. The catching of the money in the mouth of the fish was not due to his inability to pay the tax, for he clearly states that the children of the king do not pay taxes. Jesus, as the Son of God, was exempt from paying tax, because the temple was his father's own house. Jesus does not need any more opposition that would have been created by not paying the tax. The miracle then appeases the tax collectors, while re-enforcing the legal right that Jesus possessed, not to be required to pay the tax.

According to the Gospel of Mark, the KJV is unclear as to what house he was in, but in Greek, there is proof positive of that he was the owner of the house. "And again he entered into Capernaum after some days; and it was noised that he was in the house" (Mk 2:1). In Greek, this phrase is, "kai eiselthon palin eis Kapharnaoum dia emeron ekousthe oti en oika estin." This verse begins with the Greek word "kai", which means "and"; thus joining this upcoming event with the overall Gospel narrative. The word "eiselthon" means "a singular male is entering", which is referring to the subject, Jesus. The next word is the word "palin", which is an adjective that means, "back, former or re-entry"[75]. The word "eis" is a preposition that means "into" and the word, "Kapharnaoum", is the Greek name for "Capernaum". Thus, the first phrase means "And Jesus, a single male, entered back into Capernaum." The next word "dia" means, "during or through" and is a marker of an extension of time.[76] The word "emeron" means "of numerous days". The word "ekousthe" means "he was heard about", thus referring to the subject, Jesus. The word "oti" is a conjunction meaning "that", the word "en" means "in" and the word "oiko" means "a house of a singular male" or "his house". The last word "estin" is a verb that means, "right now" or "he is", referring to the single male subject, Jesus. Thus this phrase means, "through many days he was heard about that in his house he is," or better English, "after many days it was heard that

75   Frederick Danker, *A Greek – English Lexicon.* (Chicago: University of Chicago Press, 2000), 752.

76   Frederick Danker, *A Greek – English Lexicon.* (Chicago: University of Chicago Press, 2000), 224.

he (Jesus) was in his house." There is nothing in this phrase that would suggest that the house referred to belonged to anyone else except the subject, that is, Jesus.

This verse introduces the story of how the house was crowded, and four men opened a hole in the roof and let down a man sick of palsy. There is no mention of the owner protesting the destruction of the roof, or requesting compensation; that would imply someone else owned the house other than Jesus. Jesus is not upset over the hole in the roof, but is amazed at their faith and sends the man formerly sick of palsy home without asking for compensation, obviously Jesus could afford to repair the roof if the four friends did not.

Mark 9:33 reads, "And he came into Capernaum, and being in the house, he asked them." In Greek, this phrase reads, "kai elthon Kapharnaoum kia en te oika genomenos eperota autous." The Greek word "kai" means "and" thus joins the teachings of Jesus to his disciples. The word "elthon" means, "they have entered"; which is referring to the subjects, Jesus and his disciples. The word "eis" means "into" and "Kapharnaoum" is the Greek name for "Capernaum". Thus, this phrase means, "and they entered Capernaum." This phrase is joined to the next phrase by "kia" or "and". The word "en" means "in", the word "te" means "the" and the word "oikia" means "a single house". Therefore, though the subject consists of numerous people,

Jesus and the disciples, the house is a single entity. There is nothing to suggest that the house is owned by someone else, or even by one of the disciples. The translators omit reference to the group but focus on Jesus simply for clarity, because the next verse implies that disciples were present.

The next phrase, "he asked them", consists of the word "genomenos", which means "I am becoming" or "I am about to". This indicates a current action by a single male subject, Jesus. The word "eperota" is a verb that means, "to ask a question by a single male", which refers to Jesus. The word "autous" means "you" and refers to plural (numerous) males who are the object receiving the action, in this case, the disciples. Thus this phrase means, "I am about to ask you men a question." Therefore, in context, the location is Capernaum, Jesus and his disciples have arrived at a house, and Jesus is asking his disciples a question. There is no room to suggest that the house does not belong to the subject of the passage, Jesus.

According to the Gospel of John, after the marriage at Cana, Jesus moves to Capernaum. "After this he went down to Capernaum, he, and his mother, and his brethren, and his disciples: and they continued there not many days" (Jn 2:12). The Greek does not help much here. Geographically, Capernaum, is at a lower elevation than Cana, located at the shore of the Sea of Galilee. Cana was only 4 miles NE of Nazareth, and both were located on the Plain of Esdraelon. The scriptures do not indicate a reason for the move, so we can only speculate that there were more populated cities near the Sea of Galilee. A synagogue at Capernaum suggests a larger city (Mk 1:21). However, the text does imply that the mother, the brothers and the disciples were following Jesus. Traditionally, a disciple was financially dependent on the master. This would suggest that Jesus would have had to have considerable cash to provide for all those who went with him to Capernaum.

The Traditional Argument has been that Jesus was poor, totally dependent on his Heavenly Father for food daily. This argument arose from a literal interpretation of the words of Jesus, "And Jesus said unto him, the foxes have holes, and the birds of the air have nests; but the Son of man hath not where to lay his head" (Mt 8:20 & Lk 9:58).

Many have used this verse to prove their argument, that Jesus never owned property. In context, however, Jesus is responding to a scribe who approached him and said, "Teacher, I will follow you wherever you go" (v. 19). The Greek word for "scribe" is "grammateus" and is brought into English as the word "grammar". A similar word is "graphe", which comes into English as "graphite" or pencil lead, meaning, "to write".[77] Therefore, this scribe was highly educated and, as a transcriber of the writings of the law and prophets, he was also an expert on the Law of Moses. He addresses Jesus as "didaskale", which means

77   Frederick Danker, *English-Greek Lexicon*. (Chicago: University of Chicago Press, 1957), 206.

"teacher".[78] This word comes into English as "didactic" (science of teaching). Notice that he does not address Jesus as "kurios", meaning "Lord or master".[79] Jesus makes the distinction between teacher and master, "A disciple is not above his teacher, nor a slave above his master" (Mt 10:24). In Judaism, scribes were low-level officials who taught in the synagogue. They attached themselves to a rabbi until they became experts in the law themselves. This process meant that the scribe worked toward a prestigious place of honor among the religious establishment. But Jesus has no school, no synagogue and has no interest in establishing a religious institution. His disciples are called to spread the gospel with no guarantee of benefits. In the ancient world, slaves were most often the result of military victories. When all the inhabitants of a city are sold at the slave market, a wealthy landowner would purchase for himself tradespeople to build his houses, farmers to plant his crops, merchants to sell his goods, teachers to teach his children and doctors to give his family medical aid. Therefore, slaves were often very educated but they always answered to the whim of the master, never becoming his equivalent like a disciple could. Therefore, his response to the man is that though his request is noble, the man needs to seek a rabbi

---

78   Ibid, Danker, 241.

79   Ibid, Danker, 577.

rather than himself, because he has no benefits of which the man is expecting.

The reference to, "foxes having holes and birds having nests but the son of man has nowhere to lay his head", is a reference to the continual movement from town to town, not poverty. Jesus communed with the Father daily and then went about that day with the Father's instructions. In essence, Jesus was saying unlike a fox or bird that has a place to rest, he did not know where the Father would send him next. The word for "holes is "pholeos", a word used either to describe a den, lair or hole for an animal. It was also used to describe a person in the military on a campaign without shelter.[80] The word for nests is "kataskenosis", meaning a provision for shelter or constructing a shelter. In reference to birds, it means a nest.[81] Thus a fox will find an existing shelter while a bird will build their shelter. But Jesus has no place to rest his head, the word "kline" gives us the English word "recline".[82] This word, as a noun, was used of the stretcher the sick man was carried, a dining couch or a bed. The word as a verb was used to describe someone leaning over or laying down at the end of the day. The company that traveled with Jesus traveled very lightly, not carrying with

---

80   Frederick Danker, *English-Greek Lexicon.* (Chicago: University of Chicago Press, 1957), 1071.

81   Ibid, Danker, 527.

82   Ibid, Danker, 549.

themselves beds or tents like caravans did. Since the law of Moses required the taking in of strangers, Jesus and his company were able to find lodging wherever they went, so they did not have to occupy or build lodging but merely take advantage of the hospitality of others. Thus his traveling was built on the temporary hospitality of others; but that he regularly returned to Capernaum to his own home.

In conclusion, we often build whole theological arguments from a single verse. But here, the evidence from various verses does support the idea that Jesus owned a home in Capernaum. The phrase, "The foxes have holes, and the birds of the air have nests; but the Son of man has nowhere to lay his head", has nothing to do with poverty, but rather his traveling schedule.

3.   A Slave named Onesimus

The traditional view is that Onesimus was a bad slave who ran away from his master Philemon. Captured and imprisoned, he met another prisoner, the Apostle Paul. Onesimus becomes a believer in prison and ministers to Paul. The apostle in thankfulness sends the slave back to his master, requesting his master set him free. However, is this true to scripture or mere tradition?

The Scofield Study Bible says that Onesimus "had robbed his master and fled to Rome where he became a convert to Paul." Yet no verse says Onesimus was a thief. Verse 16 says, "he was unprofitable", and verse 18 says, "if he wronged you", but these are not declarations of guilt. No verse says Onesimus ran away to Rome. Verse 15 says, "he departed for a season", but does not mean he ran away. Lastly, no verse says Paul converted Onesimus. Verse 10 says, "who I have begotten in my bonds"; however this does not mean salvation or conversion.

The God's Word Study Bible says, "Onesimus, after committing theft, ran to metropolis Rome where he found Paul who converts Onesimus to Christ. Paul sends Onesimus back to Philemon and pleads Philemon to receive the penitent slave and forgive and rehabilitate Onesimus, and that Paul would make good any loss which Onesimus had caused him." Yet no verse says Onesimus was in metropolis Rome, for nowhere does the letter mention the city of Rome. No verse says Onesimus was penitent. Verse 11 says, "Onesimus is now profitable", but that does not mean he repented. Lastly, no verse says that Philemon was now to rehabilitate Onesimus.

Ellicott's Bible Commentary says that, "Paul never visited the city of Colossae", which based on Colossians 2:1 where Paul writes, "as many as have not seen my face in the flesh". However, that does not mean he had not been to the city. Ellicott's also interprets verse 16 to mean, "The slave is bought by Christ's blood and therefore becomes a brother to all who are members of the family of God." Paul, in no other epistles, ever attacks the Roman system of slavery or teaches it abolishment; he merely recognizes it as a fact of Roman society.

Carson, Moo & Morris, in their book "An introduction to the New Testament", write that "Paul was required by Roman law to send the slave Onesimus back to Philemon"; yet no verse mentions this. They also note that, "Philemon was entitled to punish his slave because a slave was considered nothing more than a living tool." Again, no verse mentions this.

John Hagee's Prophecy Study Bible says, "Onesimus was a deserter, thief, and formerly worthless slave and condemned to a violent death by Roman law"; yet no verse states this as a fact.

The One Year Bible comments about verse 13, "I really want to keep Onesimus with me in prison." No verse says that Onesimus was in prison. If Paul is sending Onesimus back to Philemon, how can one prisoner free another prisoner?

There are several problems with this traditional theory. First, nowhere does it say in Philemon that Onesimus was bad or that he ran away. Second, it does not regard the history of prisons in the ancient world. Lastly, it does not regard the history of slavery in the ancient world. To answer these questions, let's look at several things, the background to the Traditional View of Philemon, slavery in ancient Rome and prisons in ancient Rome.

Regarding the background to the Traditional View of Philemon, the traditional view that Onesimus was a runaway slave developed from the writings of the Reformers, who isolated the text from history, geography and culture, thinking they were not important. The Roman Catholic Church had elevated tradition to be equal with the Word of God. The cry of the Reformers was "Sola Scriptura", or "scripture only"; however, this only caused them to go theologically like the pendulum of a clock, from one extreme to the opposite extreme. When Martin Luther (1480-1546) translated the scriptures from Latin into German in 1530, few Bibles existed because many churches only had portions of the Bible. No Bible was divided into chapters or verses, which occurred in 1555 AD. No Bible had maps, red lettering, commentaries or references. Lastly, there were few other biblical resources such as libraries. This error was compounded by the comparison of American Black Slavery as the model for Roman Slavery. Since American slavery, as well depicted in the Shirley Temple movies and the movie "Roots", had Africans captured as slaves and brought to America to pick cotton; these slaves were rarely educated. Theologians not understanding Roman slavery imposed their modern American view of slavery on the text and automatically made three presumptions. First, that Onesimus was presumed to be a worthless, uneducated runaway and **guilty** of wrongdoing. Second, that Onesimus was presumed to be rightfully in prison. Third, that Paul asks for his freedom simply because he has sympathy for Onesimus.

Slavery is critically important in the ancient world. Just as the Egyptians had enslaved the Hebrews to build their cities, the Assyrians and Babylonians had carried the Hebrews away as slaves, so the tradition continued until Roman times. It was Julius Caesar who, as a military general in 61 BC, brought over 1 million people as slaves from Gaul (now modern France) to Rome to build his coliseums. Capturing city after city, those who resisted were killed, the able-bodied were enslaved and many others were not able to survive the forced march to Rome. Once in Rome, many were sold to the highest bidder, usually wealthy landowners would pay a high price for a doctor, lawyer, teacher or merchant. They would be paraded in their garments that indicated their education. Good prices were fetched for tradesmen, but they would have to prove both strength and skill. Fair prices were fetched for young girls who were paraded naked, sold as concubines. Caesar Augustus, with his "Lex Julia" law, recommended Roman male citizens each to have a concubine. Roman historians have written much about the custom of offering concubines to visitors as a gesture of friendship. Most of the remaining slaves spent the remainder of their lives with hard labor. Historical records indicate that about 60 percent of the population of Rome were slaves. Yet an educated slave could purchase his freedom. Caesar Augustus introduced a Roman law, which stated that slave owners were required to sell the services at a specific state price and allow a slave to keep any earnings above that state-imposed price. It was a measure to give slaves hope for freedom, which encouraged slaves to work harder. For example, if a slave sold his services to fix a roof that would take three days, he did the work, paid his master the state sum for the three days wages and kept the remainder. Caesar Augustus divided everyone into one of three classes of people. First, Roman citizens (by birth). Second, free citizens and freed citizens (former slaves). Third, the lowest class, the slaves. Slaves had no right to law, no right to marry, no right to own land. They were considered mere chattel, or property, by their masters.

Prisons in ancient Rome were like almost all things in Rome, prisons were privately managed by the highest bidder. Like taxes, which were sold to the highest bidder, these prisons were run by wealthy senators who made a profit by running a prison. Though they had to keep their prisoners alive, food was minimal and prisoners often had to do hard labor. Running a prison mirrored a slave owner, they profited by selling the labor of the criminals. Prisons were dark, cold, overrun with rats, terribly smelly from open sewers and dangerous. It was rare for a Roman citizen to be imprisoned. Most prisoners were free men who had revolted against Rome or who were thieves. Few slaves were imprisoned. If a slave ran away, slave catchers would seize the opportunity to get a reward. Those imprisoned often arranged for outside family members to bring additional food, along with clothing, medicine and bandages, because these things were not provided by the prison. If you were from a wealthier family, the outside members could pay the prison manager so that you did not have to do physical labor. You would still be incarcerated, awaiting your trial, but outside finances could make your life much more comfortable and safer.

The central verse that deals with Onesimus that would suggest in English that Onesimus was a runaway slave is verse 15, "For perhaps he therefore departed for a season, that thou shouldest receive him forever." The phrase in Greek is "tacha gar dia touto echoristhe pros oran ina aionion auton apeches." The word "tacha" means "perhaps". The word "gar" is a conjunction used to indicate a cause or reason for an action, thus it means "for this reason". The word "dia" means "through", and the word "touto" is an adjective that means "this". The word "echoristhe" means "to separate", however its form says that it was a simple past action, a one-time occurrence, and that the subject is receiving the action, not doing the action.[83] Since Onesimus is the subject of the sentence, he is receiving the action of being separated, which means that the only person who could have performed the action of separating Onesimus was Philemon. Therefore, this one verb reveals

---

83   Frederick Danker, *English-Greek Lexicon.* (Chicago: University of Chicago Press, 1957), 420.

that Philemon sent Onesimus to minister to Paul. Added together, these words say, "perhaps for this reason through this separation". The word "pros" is a conjunction that means "toward", "with", or "from". In accordance to the meaning of the sentence, it is best understood as "toward". The word "oran" is a noun that means "a short period of time", such as "an hour", or a day".[84] It often refers to a current time as when a speaker is speaking, or an event either in the past or future. Therefore, the first phrase could be translated as, "Perhaps for this reason through you separating Onesimus toward me for a short period of time." Paul now adds another phrase to give an explanation for his argument. The word "ina" is a preposition that means "in order that" and is followed by the word "aionion" that means "forever". The word "auton" means "you" and refers to Philemon, who the letter is addressed to. The word "apeches" means "desired to receive". Therefore, Philemon is expressing a desire or wish at a previous point in time in the past. This first phrase could be better translated as, "In order that as you had desired, you will receive Onesimus forever." This changes the idea of the sentence from the presumption of that Onesimus departed on his own behalf but is now returning forever to his master, to the idea that Philemon has sent his slave toward Paul for a short season in order that Philemon would receive Onesimus back forever. The

---

84   Ibid, Danker, 1102.

Greek shows that Onesimus is not a runaway slave, but a sent slave.

Another key verse is found in the Letter to the Church at Colossae. If Onesimus was sent by his master to help Paul, then we must re-examine the relationship Onesimus has with the church at Colossae, as found in Colossians. Paul writes in response to the report by Epaphras to the church at Colossae (Colossians) and specifically states that he is sending the letter with Tychicus and Onesimus. Onesimus is reported by Paul, "With Onesimus, our faithful and beloved brother, who is one of your number" (Col 4:9). This creates a problem. Some would argue that Paul is declaring Onesimus is no longer a runaway slave, but now the church is to receive him as a faithful and beloved brother who is to be treated as one of them. The other possibility is that Onesimus was a longtime member of the church of Colossae, with a reputation as a man faithful and beloved in the church at Colossae. Which is right? The Greek phrase "with Onesimus, the faithful and beloved brother who is one of you", in Greek, is "sun onesimo pisto agepeto delpho os estin exi umon". The word "sun" means "with" and the word "Onesimo" is the Greek name of Onesimus. The word "pisto" means "faithful", which comes from the root word "pistis" which means "faith".[85] It is found in Romans 1:5, "your faith is spoken of throughout the whole world." The

---

85   Frederick Danker, *English-Greek Lexicon.* (Chicago: University of Chicago Press, 1957), 818.

word "agapeto" comes from the root word "agape", which means "love". The word "delpho" means "brother". The word "os" means "who" and refers to Onesimus. This word "estin" means "is or right now". The word "exi" means "from of" and indicates a membership or belonging of a group. Lastly, the word "umon" is a pronoun that means "of you". Put together, these words mean, "With Onesimus, a faithful and loving brother who right now belongs to you." This phrase is problematic because it strongly indicates that Onesimus must be an active and well-respected member of the church at Colossae. However, some theologians have suggested that Onesimus was a faithful and beloved brother of Paul, not of the church at Colossae. Yet the subject of this sentence is the church, not Paul himself, therefore there is little support for the idea that Paul is demanding the church accept this former runaway slave as a faithful and beloved member of their community. If indeed Onesimus was a runaway slave, he would not have been an active member of the church at Colossae, and he would not be a "faithful or beloved brother".

If we look at the people Paul addresses in the letter to Philemon, and the letter he wrote to the church at Colossae, we may further be able to determine any role Onesimus may have had with the church at Colossae. Theologians generally agree that Paul had sent a letter to the church at Colossae, which he wrote in prison at Rome. Paul had been visited by Epaphras, who reports to Paul the condition of the church at Colossae. Though Colossae is a city located in the Roman Province of Asia halfway between Ephesus and Antioch of Pisidia, where Paul had been, there is no record that Paul ever visited the city. Yet Paul must have traveled through Colossae to get from Antioch to Ephesus. If upon Paul's arrival in the city he had discovered a church already there, he may have stayed just long enough to gain some friendships and move on. Since he had no part in establishing the church, he would not have listed it as a church because that would have given the wrong impression that he had a part in the establishment of the church. Thus on his third missionary journey, he may have met Colossae church leaders such as Philemon, Apphia and Archippus. Paul notes that the church meets in "thy house", but does the house refer to Philemon, Apphia or Archippus? The word "Apphia" is a woman's name, and tradition has it that she may have been the wife of Philemon. The word "delphe" is the feminine form of "delphos" and means "sister".[86] The word "Archippos" [87] is the name of the fellow soldier Archippus, and all three are considered "fellow soldiers" or comrades in arms.[88] The phrase "and from the house of yours", or better English, "and from your house" has a singular feminine dative, which suggests the house belongs

---

86   Frederick Danker, *English-Greek Lexicon.* (Chicago: University of Chicago Press, 1957), 18.

87   Ibid, Danker, 139.

88   Ibid, Danker, 979.

to the woman of the group, Apphia. Though the word "oikon" means "house", it is in a singular masculine form. [89] This may be because only men owned property. The word "ekklesia", which means "assembly", has a feminine form. It literally means "her gathering". The word "ekklesia" was also used in reference to "a regularly summoned legislative body or assembly".[90] This phrase literally means, "and from your house to her assembly". The Greek, unfortunately, is unclear in its ownership. It may be Philemon's house but a regular assembly under the leadership of Apphia. It may also be Archippos's house with Philemon's or Apphias's leadership. Though we are unclear about individual roles, it is very clear that Paul is addressing people he knows very well.

In Paul's greeting to Philemon, Paul first greets Apphia and Archipus. In the body of his message, he names Onesimus and in his final greetings, he instructs Philemon to greet, on his behalf, Epaphras, Marcus, Aristarchus, Demas and Lucas. In his greeting to the church at Colossae, he first greets the church generally but then mentions Epaphras, who has come from Colossae to report their love. In Paul's final greeting to the church in Colossae, he mentions Tychicus and Onesimus, who will tell you about everything that is happening with me (Col 4:9). Paul then

---

89   Ibid, Danker, 699.

90   Ibid, Danker, 303.

names Aristarchus, Marcus, Justus, Epaphras, Luke and Demas. The reason these salutations are important is that they show where people are located. First, both letters say Paul is in prison (but neither indicate which prison). Second, both letters say Epaphras, who came from Colossae, is with Paul. Third, both letters say Mark, Aristichus, Demas and Luke are with Paul. Fourth, both letters agree with the list of five men who are with Paul, except Philemon lists Timothy whereas Colossians lists Justus. Lastly, both letters say Onesimus is being sent by Paul from his prison, but the letter to the Colossians adds that Tychicus is accompanying Onesimus. This tells us that at least two men traveled from Colossae to see Paul in prison, they were Epaphras and Onesimus. Later, two men travel from Paul's prison to Colossae, they were Tychicus and Onesimus.

I believe that to come to the conclusion that Paul was telling the church to recognize Onesimus as a faithful and beloved brother, on the simple merit he helped Paul in prison, is conjecture only. Paul is sending Onesimus back to Philemon (v. 12) with a firm conviction his trial would be soon and that he would be released, for he asks Philemon to prepare lodging for him in Colossae (v. 22). As a dear friend, Paul says that without Philemon's agreement, he will do nothing (v. 14) regarding Onesimus, but then goes on to request that Philemon receive Onesimus back above a servant (v. 16).

Regarding the phrase, "If he (Onesimus) hath wronged thee, or oweth thee ought, put that on my account" (v. 18), there is general misunderstanding. In Greek, this phrase is, "ei de ti edikesen de e opheilei touto emoi elloga." The word, "edikesen", was used to convey "wrongdoing, to mistreat or an unjust manner".[91] It is a simple past action. The word "opheilei" was used to convey "a debt", "to owe something to someone".[92] This is a present active verb, which means the subject, Onesimus, is doing an action that is occurring now, not a past action; that is, "he is right now owing you" or "he owes you now".

Paul is not offering financial compensation for anything wrong Onesimus may have done in the distant past, which is often assumed, but rather Paul is saying that if there are any current financial obligations that Onesimus owes, that he will attend to it. Paul understands that Onesimus is owned by Philemon and is accountable to Philemon only. Paul is not saying that Onesimus was **guilty** of any wrong, but if in his conduct Philemon believes that Onesimus has not been wise in the execution of his duties, causing additional costs to Philemon, that Paul will be responsible. If Philemon trusted Onesimus to be prudent in expense and Onesimus spent much more than expected, though he did

---

91   Frederick Danker, *English-Greek Lexicon.* (Chicago: University of Chicago Press, 1957), 20.

92   Ibid, Danker, 743.

nothing wrong, it was an unexpected cost Paul was willing to reconcile.

The phase "touto emoi elloga" means "this matter we will reckon." The word "elloga" comes from the root word "ellogeo", which means, "I will make a financial charge to someone's account."[93] This is an imperative present tense verb, which means this is not a suggestion but a command that Philemon must accept any financial obligation Paul owes him regarding Onesimus.

Thus, Paul requests Philemon to prepare for him lodging (v.22). In addition, he requests that he receive Onesimus no longer as a slave, but above a servant as a brother (v.16 &17) and a partner, and as if receiving myself. The word for "partner" is "koinonon", which means "to share", "to be a companion", "to participate with", and implies an equality.[94]

In Ancient Rome, you were either a Roman citizen, a freeman (which included freedmen – those once enslaved but now free) and slaves. Slaves could purchase their freedom, but only masters could free their own slave. Paul is requesting Onesimus be granted his freedom for serving him in prison. However, being set free, as nice as that is, was of little benefit to Onesimus. As long as he had been

---

93   Ibid, Danker, 319.

94   Frederick Danker, *English-Greek Lexicon*. (Chicago: University of Chicago Press, 1957), 553.

a slave to Philemon, he had few cares because his master provided him with lodging and food. Now he would be on his own. Probably not a young man, freedom was probably a greater fear than slavery. However, the word "koinonon", which as shown meant "partner", it was possible that Paul was requesting Philemon to make Onesimus a partner in his business, giving him substantial assets.

To say that Onesimus was unprofitable does not mean that he had done anything wrong. As mentioned, masters often lent out their slaves and gained income from their labor, or if the slave worked for their master in the master's business, the master benefited accordingly. To send a slave away to tend to the needs of a fellow friend in prison meant that Philemon was not receiving the income he would have normally received for his slave. The word for "unprofitable" is "achreston" and is an adjective to describe something or someone that is not of useful benefit, it does not imply wrongdoing.[95]

I now offer a new proposal. Paul had traveled with a group of men from city to city across the Roman Provinces, establishing churches where he went. His arrest, however, meant that he was now alone. The charges against him were serious, and you took your life in your hand just to visit him in prison. Paul is now aged and no longer in good health (Phil 1:9). He would have no family help in prison, and with

---

95   Ibid, Danker, 160.

minimal finances, he could not bribe the prison officials for better treatment. Without divinely provided help, he faced the real possibility of death in prison long before getting to trial. Paul had been in jail before. He is chained in the same prison Peter had been kept (Acts 12:5), which many believe was in the fortress of Antonia in Jerusalem. Later, Paul was in the inner prison with his feet in stocks at Philippi (Acts 16:24). In Caesarea, Paul was imprisoned in Herod's castle for two years (Acts 23:25). On his way to Rome, the ship he was on shipwrecked against the Island of Melita (Acts 28:1). Three months later, the ship sailed once again to Rome. However, upon arriving at Rome, the centurion delivered the prisoners to the captain of the guard, but Paul was able to dwell by himself with a soldier keeping guard (Acts 28:16). This is very clear, while other prisoners were sent to the dungeons Paul was given the liberty to live in better surroundings and simply guarded. I believe this would have been because of his miracle-working power while at Melita, which the guards had witnessed, and the rights of his Roman citizenship. If Onesimus was in prison, he would not have had contact with Paul.

I believe that Paul had befriended a wealthy landowner, Philemon, many years before. When Philemon heard that Paul was being sent to prison, he immediately took action. Sending money would not be enough because of Paul's age and health. When you consider that it would have been foolish for a wealthy friend to send a low-level slave to help a close friend in prison, the suggestion makes little sense. He would have to send someone who was knowledgeable about health and disease, someone who could prepare food that would bring healing, someone who could treat sores or cuts. The person needed to be educated enough to negotiate with the prison manager, and someone who could read and write well. If the person brought a considerable amount of money, he could pay the prison manager to have Paul lifted out of the inner prison and set in a guarded room. A room that was warm, with a bed to sleep on, and a table to eat and write on. Paul could spend his days writing and not have to do physical labor. I believe that Philemon commissioned his own personal physician, the family doctor they had purchased years before, to travel to the prison to minister to Paul. It would have been the greatest gift he could have sent. If Onesimus was indeed a doctor, he would have had the knowledge to ensure Paul obtained the correct medicine and food to ensure the quickest physical recovery possible. In addition, the letters that Paul writes from prison indicates that Onesimus must have brought pen and paper, something extremely costly, to Paul. Paul could only have written these letters if Onesimus had brought enough money with him from Philemon to ensure Paul had better living conditions, where Paul could adequately heal from the exhaustion of being forced to march hundreds of miles to the prison. I believe that Philemon expected the worst for Paul, because all of his former imprisonments had been cruel. I believe that Onesimus may have rushed ahead of Paul and paid off the prison manager so that when Paul did arrive, he was immediately separated from the other prisoners and given a place to live by himself. Waiting for his day in court, Paul in the house was able to heal and write to the churches. He was daily visited by a company of supporters and, believing his time was at hand to appear before the court, he decides to send back Onesimus to Philemon. Paul instructs Philemon to reward Onesimus by granting him his freedom and by making him a full and equal business partner, which would give Onesimus a secure future. History records that Bishop Ignatius of Antioch in 115 AD referred to Onesimus as a former bishop of Ephesus, who had a reputation of "inexpressible love".

Paul tells Timothy to study the scriptures, not simply to read the scriptures (2 Tim. 2:15). Today, most pastors are delighted if believers would just consistently read the scriptures. Yet even pastors are often **guilty** of imposing their own worldview on scripture and come to faulty conclusions based on a lack of willingness to ask tough questions of the scriptures. Often pastors are too lazy to research more than taking the opinions of commentaries, which are often considered as thought-stoppers. My proposal is simply a probable conclusion, after searching cultural and historical clues, that might give a better understanding of the real story of Onesimus.

As we have reviewed the problems of translation, it must be remembered that the Puritans did an outstanding job considering the times. However, like every translation, the Puritans were **guilty** of motives that often enter into translation. Another factor that made a large impact on how the scriptures were translated was tradition.

Chapter 6

THE PROBLEM WITH TRADITION

T he Council of Trent (1546) was the definitive Roman Catholic response to the reformation. As part of its agenda, the Council dealt with the question of the relation of tradition and scripture, reaffirming that scripture was not the only source of revelation but tradition was a vital supplement.[96] Though the Protestants vocally protested, they soon would develop their own traditions. The previous examples of translation errors all have considerable tradition behind them, some reaching back a thousand years, and are maintained by Catholics and Protestants alike. However, there are other traditions that arose out of simple laziness. Though the scriptures clearly teach that these traditions have no merit, they persist.

1. Paul's Name

The tradition that Saul of Tarsus changed his name to Paul is not supported in scripture. Most Christians know

---

96   Alister McGrath, *The Christian Theology Reader.* (Oxford, England: Blackwell Publishers 2000), 101.

the verse, "Saul, who is also called Paul" (Acts 13:15), but this verse does not infer a change of name. The Hebrew name Saul is "Saoul", which is pronounced as "shaa-oul". The Greek name Paul is "Paulos", which is pronounced as "pow-loss". They are not the same name. So the idea that Saul is his Hebrew name and Paul is the Greek equivalent is a fallacy. Julius Caesar had imposed the law that all Roman citizens were required to have three names, the first name was Greek, the middle name was cultural and the last name indicated a region or well-established family hierarchy. By law, the apostle was given at birth the name "Paulos Saoul Tarso", or "Paul Saul Tarsus" in English. Today, you can use your middle name legally as your first name. Paul, in the company of Jews, would have used his Jewish name but, in the company of Greeks, would have used his Greek name.

2. The Date of the Birth of Jesus

The idea that Jesus was born December 25 has debated for centuries, and the general consensus has been that it was a pagan holiday the Christians chose to celebrate the birth of Jesus. Yet scripture does confirm Jesus was born at about that time. The story of the birth of Christ begins with, "And it came to pass in those days that there went out a decree from Caesar Augustus that all the world should be taxed" (Lk 2:1). Chapter 2 continues with the story of Joseph and Mary traveling to Nazareth. In context, the birth of Jesus was during the time the world was taxed. Therefore, if one knows when Rome taxed its citizens, then one would know when Jesus was born. Rome became a Republic in 504 BC and, since that time, had taxed its citizens the last week of the last month of the year. The last month of the Julian Calendar was "Decembris", or our December.[97] Epiphanius records that Christ was born the 42nd year of the reign of Octavian Augustus Caesar on the 8th day before the Ides of January, 13 days after the winter solstice, or December 25.[98] Early Church leader John Chrysostom, Bishop of Constantinople, preached that Jesus was born December 25. This is a case when the original tradition was correct, but the tradition was changed over time due to simple ignorance. The 17th century protestants were guilty of challenging traditions just because they were rejecting the established order.

3. The Day of the Crucifixion of Jesus

The idea that Jesus died on Friday and arose on Sunday is not supported by scripture. Here, simple ignorance is at play. Mark records that the day before the Sabbath, Joseph of Arimathaeas went to Pilate and asked for the body of Christ. Receiving the body of Christ, he bought fine linen and wrapped the body and laid it in a sepulchre (Mk 15:42-46).

---

97   Jack Finegan, *Handbook of Biblical Chronology.* (NJ: Princeton University Press, 1964), 76.

98   Ibid, Finegan, 258.

Taking this verse literally, the day before the Sabbath, which is Saturday, is Friday. Therefore, tradition says Jesus died on Friday; but this is not scriptural.

Barbara Bowen states there are three Sabbaths in scripture. The first Sabbath is found in Exodus 20:8, where Moses commands Israel to labor six days but rest on the seventh day. The second Sabbath is a yearly Sabbath, which is a rest for the land every seven years when no crops were planted. Then after seven of these land Sabbaths, or 49 years, the following year is a Jubilee Sabbath year, when all slaves were set free and all debt was eliminated. The third Sabbath was the festival Sabbath, which meant that festivals such as the Passover, which lasted a week, began and ended with a Sabbath (Ex 12:16; Lev. 23:7; Num. 28:16-18).[99]

The Passover was celebrated the 14th day of the first month, Nisan, of the Jewish religious year.[100] This means, like our Christmas, it is a stationary date but since there are 365 days in a year, which is not evenly divisible by 7, the day rotates each year to a different day of the week.

If the 14th day should land on a Monday, then the Passover week would begin Monday and end Monday the following week, resulting in 2 weeks where there were 2

99   Barbara Bowen, *Strange Scriptures that Perplex the Western Mind.* (Grand Rapids: Eerdmans,1987), 107.

100   Jack Finegan, *Handbook of Biblical Chronology.* (NJ: Princeton University Press, 1964), 281.

Sabbaths. The word "sabbath" simply means "rest from work".[101] Whether it was a day of rest from weekly toil, the rest of the land for a year or the time to rest from work to celebrate, it was understood by the Jews that all commerce came to an end for the duration of the Sabbath.

In the year our Lord was crucified, the first day of the Passover week began on a Thursday, meaning the Last Supper occurred on Tuesday evening. Christ stood before Pilate 6:00 AM Wednesday morning and died at 3:00 PM, the very time when the priests offered the last sacrifice. The priests killed the last lamb at 3:00 PM, because they had exactly 3 hours to roast the lamb, close down the altar and get home by 6:00 PM. Christ was the last sacrifice and, to fulfill scripture, declared, "It is finished," at precisely 3:00 PM. Christ remained in the tomb from 6:00 PM Wednesday to 6:00 PM Saturday when he arose in fulfillment of prophecy. Since Jewish days began and ended at 6:00 PM, a minute past 6:00 PM Saturday was the first moment of the first day of a new week (Sunday). Then 12 hours later, at 6AM, he met the women at the tomb. The tradition of Christ dying on Friday simply arose when someone guilty of ignorance did not know there were two Sabbaths in the week Christ was crucified. Sadly, the fallacy was perpetrated by others **guilty** of simply repeating what they learned and not testing it against scripture.

---

101   Frederick William Danker, *A Greek-English Lexicon*. (Chicago: University of Chicago Press, 2000), 908.

4. The location of Mt. Sinai

The tradition that Mt. Sinai is located in the Sinai Peninsula has no scriptural support. Howard Blum in his book, "The Gold of Exodus", recounts the modern-day discovery of the real Mt. Sinai in Saudi Arabia. Blum argued that Roman Emperor Constantine sent his mother, Helena, to find Mt. Sinai. But tired and not knowing what to look for, she picked a mountain in the Sinai Peninsula by mistake.[102] Genesis reveals that the historical boundary between Egypt and Canaan was the River of Egypt (Gen. 15:20); that the Promised Land was from the River of Egypt to the Euphrates River. The tribe of Judah had as its Southern border the River of Egypt (Josh. 15:4). After Solomon dedicates the temple, he has a great feast for all the people from Hamath to the River of Egypt (1 Kgs 8:65). The Pharaoh of Egypt marched across Judah on his way to attack Nebuchadnezzar, but King Josiah intercepted him at Megiddo, and Israel was defeated and became servant to Egypt (2 Kgs 23:29). However, Nebuchadnezzar defeated the army of Egypt so overwhelmingly that Pharaoh never came again out of his land again. Nebuchadnezzar took possession of everything that was once owned by Egypt from the river of Egypt unto the river Euphrates (2 Kgs 24:7). The Hebrew word for "river" is "minanhal", which means

---

102   Howard Blum, *The Gold of Exodus.* (New York: Simon & Schuster, 1998), 110.

"stream bed". The Nile River is never called the River of Egypt. Geological maps put the River of Egypt South of Gaza. Blum also argues that the southern part of the Sinai Peninsula was under total control of Egypt during the time of Moses because they were protecting the Pharaoh's most treasured possession – the royal mines with copper and turquoise.[103] The Sinai peninsula has been the territory of Egypt for over 6,000 years.

Moses led the children of Israel across the Strait of Tiran at the Gulf of Aquba into the land of Midian, and marches 11 miles inland to Jabal al Lawz, which is the highest mountain in Midian at 8,465 ft. This mountain has two snub-nosed peaks with a natural amphitheater-shaped slope between them. The discovery team found boundary markers consisting of piles of rocks about 4 ft. high and 8 ft. diameter, spaced evenly around the base of the mountain. They discover twelve pillar shaped altars, all in a row, which were 12 ft. in diameter with 5 ft. between them. They also discover the jewels and gold the Israelites cast down and the altar of the golden calf.

Today, much of Saudi Arabia is barren harsh desert, but at the time of Moses it was much different. The term "wilderness" (Ex 17:1) does not mean desert, it means uncultivated land. The area had a large plain of long grasses

---

103   Howard Blum, *The Gold of Exodus.* (New York: Simon & Schuster, 1998), 116.

that supported the livestock of the Israelites. Under Joshua, the Israelites would march to the Promised Land, crossing over the Jordan (Josh. 3) from the side of the territory of the Ammonites to the side of the Canaanites. If, according to most Bible maps, this is something they would not have to do because the "Wilderness of Zin" is part of the Sinai, they would have been on the Mediterranean side of the Jordan river already.

Even though there is overwhelming evidence that Mount Sinai is in ancient Midian, which is Saudi Arabia today, and not in the Sinai Peninsula, Most Christians are **guilty** of holding onto tradition rather than do the hard work of seeking the truth.

Chapter 7

THE PROBLEM WITH DENOMINATIONALISM

S tarting with the Reformers, different church bodies have defined theological words differently, often to separate themselves from other groups. However, a new trend is emerging in the 20th Century churches, which are being influenced from geography, technology and culture. The early history of the Reformation shows that early reformers that followed Luther strove to present a new body of theology that was not Catholic or Lutheran.

An example is communion. Catholics believe that the wine and bread could only be administered by a priest, as the wine and the bread undergo a metaphysical change to become the literal blood and body of Christ (transubstantiation). Luther argued that communion did not need to be served by priests, and that the body and blood are present in the bread and wine (consubstantiation). Calvin argued that Christ is present spiritually and not physically, but the bread and wine only spiritually nourish the participant. The Zwinglian view is that communion is a commemoration of the Lord's death and, therefore, the bread and wine are only symbolic.[104] It would appear from history, therefore, that in a rush to define their own theology, in a desire to be different on all points, they were somewhat creative.

In addition, many of these leaders redefined theological terms. However, they did not redefine the word "sin", and so all churches remain with a similar viewpoint of sin. Though Martin Luther correctly rejected the sale of indulgences and penance because the value of the penance depended on the wealth of the believer, he unfortunately went too far and threw out the baby with the bathwater. That is why Protestants generally have a lower perception of the seriousness of sin, because there is no concept of payment and no concept of Purgatory, where one atones for their sin. For many Protestants, salvation is for the asking. Since we believe that Jesus died for all our sins, this has propagated the belief that no sin is too serious. However, at the same time, we like to hold over the unbelievers that the least sin will send the sinner to hell as easily as the greatest sin.

Moe argues that culture and geography of a region have more influence on the beliefs and behavior of parishioners

104   Millard Erickson, *Christian Theology*. (Grand Rapids: Baker Books, 2000),1115 – 1129.

than the denomination has.[105] With the tremendous growth of technology, cultural ideas that were once isolated can be brought into the home by the click of a mouse. Syncretism is nothing new to the church. In Barbados, voodoo is common: it is 50 percent Catholicism and 50 percent witchcraft. But few Christians understand that yoga is a well-defined, centuries-old form of Buddhist worship. What is portrayed as beneficial exercise is pagan worship that opens the spirit of the person to satanic oppression. Moe talks of how pastors are masters of denial, for when pastors accept the doctrines and traditions of their denomination, they are required to deny certain things as a result of those doctrines.[106] I know a former Baptist minister who received the Pentecostal Holy Spirit baptism with the evidence of speaking in tongues. The pastor, in her zeal, shared with her congregation the doctrine of speaking in tongues and was immediately fired. The pastor had violated denominational protocol. I certainly hurt for pastors who teach things that they know in their heart are not scriptural, but must maintain denominational protocol.

In summary, however a person chooses to believe or not believe the above research addendums means little, they were presented with one purpose, that it can be established

---

105   Kenneth Alan Moe, *The Pastor's Survival Guide*. (Bethesda, MD: Alban Institute Publication, 2001), 10.

106   Ibid, Moe, 73.

that the King James version is not inerrant. As a translation, it has errors. With this conviction, I can now proceed upon a basis of this study that the only manner in which an accurate understanding of Hebraic concept of sin can be created is to examine the Hebrew OT words for sin and then compare them with the Greek NT words for sin. Since nowhere in scripture are these words clearly defined, definition must come from context.

It is my conviction that in the Hebraic system, there are three general categories that all sins can be placed under; unforgivable sins, forgivable sins and relational sins. Elwell argues that sin not only has a vast terminology, but within its biblical contexts suggests that sin has three aspects, breach of law, violation of relationships with people and rebellion against God.[107] Elwell's definition is correct as an overall concept, but Israel was the only covenant community with the law where breach of the law was possible. Paul clearly states it is not possible to breach a law you have no understanding of. Yet just as Adam's sin was rebellion toward God, so people outside the covenant rebelled in their knowledge of God, for all men come from one family. Sin and the atonement for sin was clearly established before the law of Moses. In the Hebraic system, the understanding of sin was central in their community life, because every sin was atoned for by different means; death, a cereal offering

107   Walter A. Elwell, *Baker Theological Dictionary of the Bible.* (Grand Rapids: Baker Books, 1996), 737.

or the shedding of blood of an animal sacrifice. The Lord put to death the two sons of Judah, Er and Onan, because they were evil (Gen. 38:7-10). Cain brought a cereal offering before the Lord (Gen. 4:3) and Noah offered a burnt offering (Gen. 8:20). However under Moses, sin would finally be defined by a sacrificial system that set clear parameters of conduct.

However, the movement in the 3rd century to fully set Christianity in a different direction than Judaism, much of the understanding of how the Jews understood sin was lost to the Christian church. Therefore, the next three chapters look at the three general categories of sins as understood by the Hebrews.

Chapter 8

THE UNFORGIVABLE SINS

D elitzsch argued that there are twelve specific sins denounced in the Mosaic Law, which incur the extreme penalty of death. For these sins, there is no sacrifice; once you were found **guilty** before the judges, you were taken out and stoned. Many of these sins originated outside Israel in the nations that surrounded Israel. For the Israelite who committed these sins, they plainly placed themselves outside the covenant and bore appropriate punishment.

I have selected four Hebrew words, which frame the concept of unforgivable sins. These are the sin of apostasy, the sin of evilness, the sin of wickedness and the sin of abomination.

1.   The Unforgivable Sin of Apostasy

Apostasy from God toward the service of other gods is denounced as the extremist breach of the law possible (Deut. 18:9-12). The reason apostasy is such a severe breach is that in the ancient world, there was no concept of what Americans call separation of church and state. In the same manner that in Muslim countries, Shria law dictated every facet of life including all levels of government; so Mosaic Law dictated every facet of life for the Israelite. Mosaic law was a covenant between Israel and Yahweh. There are numerous covenants in the scriptures. Covenants are legal agreements that bind individuals or social groups, they can be unilateral or bilateral, conditional or unconditional, temporary or permanent.[108] Some are between God and man (Abrahamic, Mosaic, Davidic), covenants between kings and subjects (vassal covenants) and covenants between people (treaties by marriage).

Israel was surrounded by ancient societies, which likewise revolved around the worship of gods. Solomon built places of worship for Ashtoreth, the goddess of the Zidonians; Milcom, the god of the Ammonites; Chemosh, the god of Moab; and Molech, the god of the Ammonite (1 Kgs 11:5-7). The Ten Commandments directly forbid many of the practices of these religions, including child sacrifice (Lev. 20:2), bestiality (Ex 22:19), incest (Lev. 20:11,12), homosexuality (Lev. 20:13), witchcraft (Ex 22:18), slavery (Ex 21:16) and astrology (Deut. 17:3). Israel's failure to keep separate from the gods of the surrounding nations eventually brought great punishment. Doorly argues that Baalism was carried on in the temple of Jerusalem from the

---

108   Guy Duty, *God's Covenants and Our Time.* (Minneapolis, Minnesota: Bethany Fellowship Printing, 1964), 5-10.

time of Manasseh (2 Kgs 21:3) to the reforms of Josiah (2 Kgs 23:6), indicating that Baalism had moved from hillside shrines to temples within the city of Jerusalem and finally infiltrated into the temple site itself.[109] In addition, there is also reference to "the host of heaven", which Doorly believes refers to the twelve signs of the Zodiac (2 Kgs 23:5). Ezekiel said the Lord would lay the dead carcasses of the children of Israel before their idols and that he would scatter their bones round about their idol altars (Ezek 6:5).

The Hebrew word for apostasy is the word "mesubah" (pronounced as "meugh-shoe-vah"). It occurs 13 times in the OT and is often translated as "backsliding". The key verse is found in Jeremiah that defines the apostasy of Israel as having gone up upon every high mountain, under every green tree and played the harlot (Jer. 3:6). Jeremiah tells the Israelites their own apostasy is an evil and bitter thing, for they have forsaken the Lord and his fear is not in them (Jer. 2:19). Jeremiah also uses the allegory of marriage to claim that in apostasy Israel committed adultery, but though the Lord had given her a bill of divorce, yet her treacherous sister Judah feared not but went and played the harlot also (Jer. 3:8). In this state of apostasy, Israel had justified herself more than Judah (Jer. 3:11). Jeremiah then warns of the penalty of apostasy with the allegory of a lion out of the forest will kill them, a wolf in the evening will spoil them and

---

109   William Doorly, *Prophet of Love: Understanding the Book of Hosea.* (New York: Paulist Press, 1991), 89.

a leopard will watch over their cities that anyone that goes out will be torn in pieces because their apostasies (Jer. 5:6). Yet after all his warnings, a weary Jeremiah laments that the people of Jerusalem slid back by a perpetual apostasy and continued to hold fast onto deceit refuse to return to the Lord (Jer. 8:5). Jeremiah is not all judgment; for he declares the Lord will be merciful if they return from their apostasy and he will heal their apostasy (Jer. 3:22). This is echoed by Hosea, who also declared that though his people are bent to apostasy (Hos 11:7), the Lord will heal their apostasy and he will love them freely; for his anger is turned away (Hos 14:5).

Clearly, the heart of the Lord is to show mercy; yet it is conditional upon repentance. Only when repentance fails must judgment come. Bruner argues that it had become common in Israel to think of forgiveness as "God forgives three times and punishes the fourth." This is found in Amos, "for three transgressions of ... and for four" (Am 1:3-15). The Lord announced judgment on several nations on the fourth transgression, having not punished the first three.[110] When King Hezekiah showed the Babylonians all of the treasures of the temple, he was sharply rebuked by Isaiah (2 Kgs 20:12-19). Hezekiah was content to know there would be peace as long as he lived, even if everything would be carried away after his death. Israel had become

---

110   Frederick Bruner, *Matthew: A Commentary.* (Grand Rapids: Eerdmans, 2004), 236.

complacent, the sins of today could be paid for by a future generation; they only cared for the present. Yet that day came, and Israel would return from the Babylonian captivity to never apostatize again.

The Greek word for apostasy is "apostrepo" (pro-nounced "awe-poss-tree-fow"). It literally means "I turn away by rejecting, repudiating."[111] It occurs 9 times in the NT. Pilate said to the chief priests that they had brought Jesus before him as one that turned away (apostasy) the people but after he had examined Jesus, Pilate found no fault in him according to their accusations (Lk 23:14). In Peter's second sermon, Peter tells the Jews that God sent his son Jesus to them before the Gentiles to bless them by turning away (apostate) every one of them from their ungodliness (Acts 3:26). Paul, in his letter to the Church at Rome, declared that all Israel will be saved because it was written there shall come out of Zion the Deliverer who will turn away (apostate) all ungodliness from Jacob (Rom 11:26). Yet to Timothy, Paul warns about the apostates, that they will turn away (apostate) their ears from the truth and shall be turned (apostate) unto fables (2 Tim. 4:4). The writer to the Hebrews warns them not to refuse he that speaks, for if they escaped not who refused him that spoke on earth,

---

111   Frederick William Danker, *A Greek-English Lexicon.* (Chicago: University of Chicago Press, 2000), 122.

much more shall not we escape if we turn away (apostate) from him that speaks from heaven (Heb 12:25).

F. F. Bruce argued that blasphemy against the Holy Ghost is tantamount to apostasy, and that it is impossible to renew apostates to repentance (Heb 6:4), since they have repudiated the only way to salvation. Bruce also said that to slander the Son of God while Jesus ministered was for-givable, because the identity of the Son of God was veiled in his humanity and might easily fail to recognize him for who he was.[112]

In summary of apostasy, the Israelites thought that they could worship the gods of other nations alongside of Yahweh; but Yahweh called it apostasy, and they paid a horrible price in Babylonian captivity. They were directly forbidden to be involved in the practices of these religions, which included child sacrifice, bestiality, incest, witchcraft, homosexuality, slavery and astrology. They had rejected and even repudiated the commandments of the Lord. For Gentile Christians, they would also have to learn that apostasy carried a terrible price, for to apostate the Gospel meant loss of eternal life as they ran after fables. Apostasy occurs when someone is **guilty** of repudiating what they have learned about the love of Christ.

---

112   F.F. Bruce, *The Hard Sayings of Jesus.* (Downers Grove, Illinois: InterVarsity Press, 1983), 92.

2.   The Unforgivable Sin of Evilness

This sin is represented by the Hebrew word "ra" (pronounced as "rah"). This word is mentioned 299 times in the OT and is associated with three other words developed from the same root word. The word "ra'a" (pronounced "raw-awe") is a verb that means, "to break". The word "ra'ats" (pronounced "raw-ats") is a verb that means, "to shatter". The word "ra'ash" (pronounced "raw-ash") is a verb that means, "to shake". Therefore, unlike apostasy, which was a turning away, evilness goes further because it has a component of violence.

It is first mentioned after Adam and Eve ate of the fruit. The Lord said man has become like one of us knowing good and evil (Gen. 3:22). After the flood, God declared he would not again curse the ground because the curse had come because the imagination of a man's heart, which is evil from his youth (Gen. 8:21). The men of Sodom were wicked (evil) before the Lord exceedingly (Gen. 13:13). Judah took a wife of the Canaanites who bore him his first son, Er, but he was so wicked (evil), the Lord slew him (Gen. 38:7). After Moses came down from the mountain with the tablets and saw the people dancing around the golden calf, Aaron said the people are set on mischief (evil) (Ex 32:22). The children of Israel strip themselves of their ornaments after hearing that they would not go into the promised land, but die in the wilderness. They mourned when they heard the evil tidings (Ex 33:4). It is not that the judgment or message was evil, but that the consequence was equivalent to the punishment of evil, death.

The people complain to Moses about the wilderness conditions, that he has brought them up out of Egypt to an evil place where there was no place to seed, no fig trees, no grape vines or water to drink (Num. 20:5). Their perception was the wilderness was evil because a person could easily die there. A whole generation died in the wilderness, because the Lord's anger was kindled against Israel. He made them wander in the wilderness forty years, until all the generation that had done evil in the sight of the Lord was consumed (Num. 32:13). However, their children, who had no knowledge between good and evil, would grow to be adults and enter the promised land (Deut. 1:39). The Lord covenants to take away from them all sickness and will not put the evil diseases of Egypt upon them (Deut. 7:15). Disease is not evil in itself, but disease is evil because of its source. Moses calls any prophet or seer evil that teaches them to go after other gods and commands them to be put to death (Deut. 13:5). Likewise, an idol worshipper commits evil and is commanded to be put to death (Deut. 17:5). The adulterer and adulteress commit evil and are to be put to death (Deut. 22:23). If an Israelite steals another Israelite and sells him into slavery, he is called evil and is to be put to death (Deut. 34:8). Probably the greatest heartbreak of

Moses was his final words, that the people of Israel after he dies will become evil (Deut. 32:30). That is why Moses said, "I have set before you this day life and good, and death and evil" (Deut. 30:15).

Israel, during the period of the Judges, became evil by serving the gods of Baal (Judg. 2:11). The sons of the prophet Eli were evil because they lay with the women who assembled at the door of the tabernacle. Eli told them he had heard of their evil and told his sons that if a man sins against another man, a judge would judge him; but if a man sins against the Lord, no man can help him (1 Sam. 2:22-25). Therefore, the nature of evil is against the Lord. The failure of King Saul to obey the Lord and kill King Amelek was an evil that cost him this throne (1 Sam. 15:19).

David's arrangement of the death of Uriah was evil (2 Sam. 12:9). Solomon prays for wisdom to judge his people and discern between good and evil (1 Kgs 3:9). The idolatry of Solomon was evil, for he worshipped Astoreth, the goddess of the Zidonians, and Milcom, the abomination of the Ammonites (1 Kgs 11:6). The phrase, "did evil in the sight of the Lord", would be the actions of many of the kings of Judah and Israel.

Job was a man that was perfect and upright, one that feared God and who turned aside evil (Job 1:1). Eliphaz tells Job that the Lord would deliver him from death in seven troubles (sickness, famine, war, false accusation, adversity, wild beasts and sin), because evil could not touch him (Job 5:19). Yet Job witnessed how evil came and cost him his family's lives.

One of the best-known psalms is, "Yea though I walk through the valley of death, I will fear no evil for you are with me, your rod and your staff they comfort me" (Ps 23:4). David cries about those evil people who want to kill him, who gather themselves together, they hide themselves, they mark my steps and they wait for my soul (Ps 56:6). There is some literary license here: their evil is to kill, to wait for a man's soul. The Psalmist asks of the Lord that he would give him rest from the days of adversity (evil) until the pit is dug for the wicked (Ps 94:13). You that love the Lord are to hate evil, for the Lord preserves the souls of his saints, he delivers them out of the hands of the wicked (Ps 97:10). Whosoever causes the righteous to go astray in an evil, he shall fall himself into his own pit (Prv. 28:10).

Isaiah speaks of how Jerusalem was the Lord's vineyard, but it brought forth wild grapes because they called evil, good and good, evil. They called darkness, light and light, darkness; and they called bitter, sweet and sweet, bitter (Isa. 5:20). Isaiah also calls men evil who devises evil devices to destroy the poor (Isa. 32:7). Opposite are the righteous who despises the gain of oppressors, who shakes his hands from holding bribes, who stops his ears from hearing of murder plots and shuts his eyes from seeing evil (Isa. 33:15). This is repeated in the phrase, "their feet run to evil, and they make haste to shed innocent blood" (Isa. 59:7).

Jeremiah accused the priests of setting up idols in the temple, declaring, "It was evil when they set up an abomination in the house to pollute it" (Jer. 7:30). Jeremiah, with his sign of a girdle, calls Judah an evil people who refuse to hear the words of the Lord, but walk after other gods to serve them and to worship them (Jer. 13:10). After the fall of Jerusalem, some of the remnants come to Jeremiah declaring that whether it was good or evil, they would obey the voice of the Lord (Jer. 42:6). Since leaving the region was punishable by death (evil), these people were making a declaration that whether they enjoy peace or death, they will obey the Lord.

In exile, Ezekiel declared to Israel that they would remember their own evil, that their doings were not good and they would loathe themselves in their own sight for their iniquities and their abominations (Ezek 36:31).

Amos declared, "Seek good and not evil that you might live, and the Lord, the God of hosts will be with you" (Amos 5:14). Micah speaks of the horror of cannibalism that was central to idol worship because they hated good and loved evil, flaying the skin off their victims, plucking off their flesh from off the bones of their victims and then also eating the flesh (Mic. 3:2-3). Zephaniah prophecies that when Israel comes back to her land, they will have no more evil, the

Lord will be in the midst of them and you shall not even see evil (Zeph. 3:17). This is a promise of safety from violence.

This sin of evilness is represented by the Greek word "poneros" (pronounced "poe-nee-ross) and occurs 78 times in the NT. Jesus told his disciples that they are blessed when men would revile them, persecute them, and shall say all manner of evil against them, falsely for his sake (Matt. 5:11). Jesus warned that communication was to be "Yea, Yea, Nay, Nay", for whatsoever is more than these comes of evil (Matt. 5:37). We are children of the Father in heaven who makes his sun to rise on the evil and on the good, and sends rain on the just and on the unjust (Matt. 5:45). The Lord ends his prayer with, "And lead us not into temptation; but deliver us from evil, for yours is the kingdom, and the power, and the glory forever" (Matt. 6:13). Jesus declared an evil eye fills the whole body full of darkness (Matt. 6:23). Jesus told the people that if they being evil know how to give good gifts unto their children, how much more will their Father in heaven give good things to them that ask him (Matt. 7:11)? Every good tree brings forth good fruit, but every corrupt tree brings forth evil fruit (Matt. 7:17) and that is why you, being evil, cannot speak good things because out of the abundance of the heart, the mouth speaks (Matt. 12:34). When asked for a sign, Jesus declared that an evil and adulterous generation seeks after a sign, and there shall no sign be given to it, but the sign of the prophet Jonah (Matt. 12:39). It is not surprising Jesus calls spirits, evil; that when cast out, the spirit takes with himself seven other spirits more evil than himself, and the last state of the man is worse than the first (Matt. 12:45). Jesus taught that when anyone hears the word of the kingdom, and understands it not, then comes the wicked (evil) one and catches away that which was sown in his heart (Matt. 13:19). The field is the world; the good seed are the children of the kingdom; but the tares are the children of the wicked (evil) one (Matt. 13:38). So shall it be at the end of the world; the angels will come and separate the wicked (evil) ones from among the just (Matt. 13:49). In the parable of the wicked servant, the master called the servant to account calling him a wicked (evil) servant, for he forgave him of a great debt, but the evil servant could not forgive a small debt (Matt. 18:32). Likewise, in the parable of the tal-ents, the lord calls his servants to account for their talents, but to the last one the master called him an wicked (evil) and slothful servant, because he knew his master reaped where he had not sown and gathered where he had not cut down (Matt. 25:16). In the parable of the marriage feast, the king found those called to the feast unworthy, so he sent his servants to go into the highways and gather as many as they could find, both bad (evil) and good, and the wedding was furnished with guests (Matt. 22:9).

Luke said of all the wickedness (evil) that Herod the tetrarch had done, yet above all that he shut up John in prison (Lk 3:19,10). Luke also calls evil spirits wicked spirits, stating that Jesus, in that same hour, cured many of their infirmities and plagues, sent out wicked spirits, and many that were blind received sight (Lk 7:21).

John begins his writing with a condemnation, that light is come into the world, and men loved darkness rather than light, because their deeds were evil (Jn 3:19). John records the last prayer of Jesus, that his Father not take them out of the world, but that he keep them from evil (Jn 17:15).

When Paul and Timothy come to Thessalonica, Jews that believed not moved with envy took certain lewd (evil) fellows of the baser sort: gathered a company, set all the city in an uproar, assaulted the house of Jason and sought to bring Paul and Timothy out to the crowd to hurt them (Acts 17:5). When Paul stood before Gallio, Gallio said to the Jews that if it were a matter of wrong or wicked (evil) lewdness, then he would hear their case against Paul (Acts 18:14). Paul later testifies that before Festus that when his accusers stood up, they were not able to accuse him of such (evil) things (Acts 25:18). As Paul awaits in Rome for his trial, he was told that they had not received letters from Judaea about him nor had those from Judaea willing to speak any harm (evil) about Paul (Acts 28:21). Paul encourages the church at Rome to let love be without dissimulation, abhor that which is evil and cleave to that which is good (Rom 12:9). To the Church at Corinth, Paul warns of their immorality. They that are without God, he will judge; but you must judge that wicked (evil) person and put him away from among yourselves (1 Cor 5:13). Jesus gave himself for our sins that he might deliver us from this present evil world, according to the will of God our Father (Gal. 1:4). Therefore, we are to put on the whole armor of God, taking the shield of faith, wherewith you will be able to quench all the fiery darts of the wicked (evil) one (Eph 6:16). To the church in Thessalonica, Paul urges them to abstain from all appearance of wickedness (evil) (1 Thes 5:22). By the faithfulness of God, they will be delivered from unreasonable and wicked (evil) men; for all men do not have faith (2 Thes 3:2). Paul sends a similar message to Timothy, that though evil men and seducers will wax worse and worse, deceiving and being deceived (2 Tim. 3:13); yet the Lord will deliver us from every evil work (2 Tim. 4:18).

The writer to the Hebrews warns the brethren, lest there be in any of you an evil heart of unbelief, in departing from the living God (Heb 3:12). But let us draw near with a true heart in full assurance of faith, having our hearts sprinkled from an evil conscience, and our bodies washed with pure water (Heb 10:22).

James rebukes the believers, charging them of being partial, becoming judges of evil thoughts (Jas 2:4); yet you rejoice in your boastings, but all such rejoicing is evil (Jas 4:16).

The Apostle John makes three references to the word evil: you have overcome the wicked (evil) one (1 Jn 2:13). You are not like Cain, who was of that wicked (evil) one, and slew his brother (1 Jn 3:12). He that is begotten of God keeps himself, and that wicked (evil) one touches him not (1 Jn 5:18).

Carnell argues that evil is anything that frustrates human values, and that there are two kings of evil, natural and moral. Natural evils include disasters of hurricanes and floods, whereas moral evils can be mental, such as lust and fear, or physical, such as martyrdom.[113] Genesis declares that Yahweh created the world in six days and that everything he made was very good (Gen. 1:31). Though the world would undergo a flood and separation of the continents (Gen. 10:25), it remains good. Weather patterns are neither good or bad, and though Yahweh has used earthquakes and other natural forces to cause men to repent, the forces in themselves are neither good or evil. Therefore, I reject the argument that natural disasters are evil, and maintain that evil is strictly a function of a free will and cannot be attributed to inanimate objects or powers, such as the wind.

In summary, the word "evil" is violence that is of the heart. For some, it began with a straying from the Lord to other gods, but maturing with the horrible acts they did for those other gods, which included slavery, murder, child sacrifice and fornication. For others, their evil consisted of corruption and the invention of devices to hurt others. Those who were evil had no judge to correct them, only to judge them. In the

---

113   Edward J. Carnell, *An Introduction to Christian Apologetics.* (Grand Rapids: Eerdmans, 1948), 280.

New Testament, the word seams less harsh until you are reminded that that entire generation perished in 70 AD for their evil, in fulfillment of the words of Jesus. I once worked with a "white witch" who was very proud that she was able to use her spiritual powers to help people and would never consider using her powers to hurt people. Here is someone who started the pathway to witchcraft by first repudiating the Christian ethic, therefore she is **guilty** of apostasy, but has not crossed over into violence and is not yet **guilty** of evilness.

3.   The Unforgivable Sin of Wickedness

The sin of wickedness is expressed by the Hebrew word "rasa" (pronounced as "raugh-shaw"). It occurs 242 times in the OT and is defined as "criminal, **guilty** of death". [114] One of the best known verses of the wicked is, "As I live, says the Lord God, I have no pleasure in the death of the wicked but that the wicked turn from his way and live; for why will you die?" (Ezek 33:11).

The first OT narrative about the wicked is the intercession Abraham has before the Lord for Sodom, asking if the Lord would destroy the righteous with the wicked (Gen. 18:23). Pharaoh confessed unto Moses that he had sinned, the Lord was righteous and he and his people are wicked (Ex

---

114   F. Brown, S. Driver, C. Briggs, *The Brown-Driver-Briggs Hebrew and English Lexicon*, (Peabody, Mass.: Hendrickson, 2003), 959.

9:27). Moses taught the Israelites not to raise a false report, neither put their hand with the wicked, to be an unrighteous witness (Ex 23:1). The Lord declares that they were to keep far from a false matter, though the innocent and righteous may not kill you, yet I will not justify your wickedness (Ex 23:7). The friends of Job speak of the wicked; the eyes of the wicked will fail, they will not escape and their hope shall be as the giving up of the ghost (Job 11:20). The light of the wicked shall be put out (Job 18:5). Zophar speaks of the heritage of the wicked as something forever lost (Job 20).

This word does not occur in Leviticus because there is no sacrifice for wickedness, only the death penalty. Moses spoke to Israel about Dathan and Abirim, telling the congregation to depart from the tents of those wicked men and touch nothing of theirs, lest they be consumed in these men's sins (Num. 16:26). Regarding disputes, if there was a controversy between two men and they came before the judges, the judges would justify the righteous and condemn the wicked (Deut. 25:1). Condemnation was nothing less than the penalty of death.

Hannah praises the Lord with the confession that the Lord will keep the feet of his saints but the wicked will be silent in darkness, for by strength will no man prevail (1 Sam. 2:9).

When David cut the hem off of Saul's robe, he quoted a proverb of the ancients that declares wickedness proceeds from the wicked; but my hand will not be upon you (1 Sam.

24:13). David told the men who killed Saul's son that they were much more wicked than someone who killed a righteous person in his own house, upon his own bed, therefore he would require his blood by their hands (2 Sam. 4:11). When Solomon dedicated the temple, he prayed the Lord in heaven to judge his servants with condemning the wicked by bringing his way upon his own head, but to justify the righteous by giving him according to his righteousness (1 Kgs 8:32).

This is echoed by Isaiah, who says it shall be ill with the wicked, for he will receive the reward of his wicked hands (Isa. 3:12). Isaiah declared the word of the Lord that he will punish the world for their evil and the wicked for their iniquity (Isa. 13:11). Isaiah also declared that if favor is shown to the wicked, they will not learn righteousness. Even in a land of uprightness, they will deal unjustly and cannot behold the majesty of the Lord (Isa. 26:10). Isaiah defined the wicked like the troubled sea when it cannot rest, whose waters cast up mire and dirt (Isa. 57:20). Thus the wicked are not inclined to change, resulting in forever cut off of the presence of the Lord, but to a wicked person, there remains a glimmer of hope by means of repentance. If the wicked forsake their way, and the unrighteous their thoughts, and return unto the Lord, the Lord will have mercy upon them for he will abundantly pardon (Isa. 55:7).

Jeremiah, who faced great trials at the hands of wicked leaders, declared that among his people were wicked men who lay in wait, setting snares to trap and catch others (Jer. 5:26).

The Lord, by Ezekiel, warns pastors who are watchman over the souls of men that when the Lord tells them to warn the wicked that they will die, and they do not warn the wicked to save his life, that wicked man will die in his iniquity, but his blood the Lord will require at the hand of the watchman (Ezek 3:18). The Lord speaks of the judgment coming upon the land of Israel that he will give it into the hands of strangers for a prey, and to the wicked of the earth for a spoil; and they shall pollute it (Ezek 7:21).

The prophet Habakkuk speaks of dispersed Israel because the law was slacked, judgment never went forth because the wicked had compassed about the righteous, resulting in wrong judgments proceeding (Hab. 1:4).

Referring to the key verse for wickedness, "I have no pleasure in the death of the wicked," the LXX interprets the word "wicked" as "asebes". It often translated as "ungodly", which is found 282 times in the LXX, but only 9 times in the NT. The word "asebes" (pronounced "awe-see-bess) means, "to act with impiety, or violate norms for proper relation to deity, irreverent, ungodly."[115] This word is not found in the Gospels, but is used by Paul, Peter and Jude. The Puritans used the word "wicked" in the Gospels, because they believed the Jews were wicked.

---

115   Frederick William Danker, *A Greek-English Lexicon.* (Chicago: University of Chicago Press, 2000), 141.

Paul argues justification by faith that he who comes to God not by works, but believes on him that justifies the ungodly (wicked), his faith is counted for righteousness (Rom 4:5). Paul also declares that when we were yet sinners, in due time Christ died for the ungodly (wicked) (Rom 5:6). Paul, speaking of the Law of Moses, the law was not made for a righteous person, but for the lawless, the disobedient, the ungodly (wicked), the sinners, those unholy or profane and for murderers (1 Tim. 1:10).

Peter argues that we are to cease from sin, for if the righteous are scarcely saved, where will the ungodly (wicked) and the sinners go (1 Pet. 4:18)? God spared not the old world, but saved Noah, a preacher of righteousness, and brought the flood upon the world of the ungodly (wicked) (2 Pet. 2:5). God turned the cities of Sodom and Gomorra into ashes, making them examples to those that would live ungodly (wickedly), but delivered Lot who had been vexed with the filthy conversation of the wicked. For as Lot dwelt among them, he was vexed by seeing and hearing daily their unlawful (wicked) deeds (2 Pet. 2:6-8). The heavens and the earth are reserved unto fire against the Day of Judgment of ungodly (wicked) men (2 Pet. 3:7). Jude writes to encourage believers to contend for the faith after certain men crept in, unawares who were before of old ordained to this condemnation. Ungodly (wicked) men turned the grace of our God into lasciviousness, and denied the only

Lord God and our Lord Jesus Christ (Jude 1:4). The Lord is coming with tens of thousands of his saints to execute judgment upon all, and to convince all that are ungodly (wicked) among them of their ungodly (wicked) deeds, which they have ungodly (wickedly) committed (Jude 1:15).

In summary, there is severe judgment against those who are wicked, but unlike those who commit apostasy and those who are evil, there seems to be an olive branch by the Lord who will pardon wickedness. The central core of wickedness is lawlessness. The problem is that those who are wicked are so inclined toward their wickedness that they spurn any mercy. Therefore, Jesus is in harmony with the prophets, that wickedness comes with a terrible penalty. Just as the prophets witnessed the destruction of Samaria in 701 BC and the fall of Jerusalem in 586 BC, the apostles would witness the fall of Jerusalem in 70 AD in fulfillment of the judgment of Christ for their wickedness.

However, there is a verse that stands in contrast: Paul writing to the Corinthian believers that though they were at one time alienated and enemies in your mind by wicked works, yet now has Christ reconciled (Col 1:21). How is it that the Jews were horribly punished for wickedness, yet the Gentiles spared and even reconciled? The answer lies in the concept of covenant. Jews who make the willful choice to do wickedness do so in full awareness of their actions, breaching the law of Moses. Though Corinth had numerous temples and were famous for their wickedness,

Paul declares to the new believers who have now left the temple prostitution lifestyle and converted to Christ that their former wickedness was forgiven and they were reconciled to God. I attribute that their wickedness was done in ignorance and not rebellion toward God, for they did not have the law of God. They were **guilty** of lawlessness, rejecting the lawful ordinances by the state.

4.   The Unforgivable Sin of Abomination

This sin is represented by the Hebrew word "tobabat" (pronounced as "tove-ee-vath"). It is found 118 times in the OT and is often translated as "detestable". The first instance of this word occurs when the ten brothers eat in front of Joseph, the Egyptians would not eat bread with the Hebrews, for that was an abomination unto the Egyptians (Gen. 43:33). This was because Hebrews kept sheep. Pharaoh told Moses they could sacrifice in Egypt, but Moses said to Pharaoh that they could not because they would sacrifice the abomination of the Egyptians and, therefore, they needed to go three days journey into the wilderness, otherwise if we sacrifice before the eyes of the Egyptians, they will stone us (Ex 8:26,27).

The word is used to describe defilement. Moses said that for the abominations have the men of the land of Canaan done, which were before you, leaving the land defiled. That the land not also spew you out, when you defile it, as it spewed out the nations before you, because he who commits any of these abominations, even that soul will be cut off from among the people (Lev. 18:27-29).

During the reign of the kings, there were high places that Solomon built for Ashoreth, the abomination of the Zidonians, and for Chemosh, the abomination of the Moabites, and for Milcom, the abomination of the children of Ammon (2 Kgs 23:13). During the reign of Rehoboam, there were sodomites in the land who did according to all the abominations of the nations, which the Lord cast out before the children of Israel (1 Kgs 14:24). King Josiah took away all the abominations out of all the countries that pertained to the children of Israel, and made all that were present in Israel to serve the Lord (2 Chr 34:33). Yet Ezra said the people of Israel, the priests and the Levites had not separated themselves from the people of the lands, doing according to their abominations of the Canaanites, Hittites, Perizzites, Jebusites, Egyptians and the Amorites (Ezr 9:1).

However, Moses would use this word to describe detestable sins. Regarding homosexuality, you cannot lie with mankind as with womankind; it is an abomination (Lev. 18:22). Regarding idolatry, idols were to be destroyed, even the gold and silver could not be re-smelted, lest they be snared therein, for it is an abomination to the Lord your God (Deut. 7:25). Child sacrifice was an abomination the Lord hated, for even their sons and their daughters they have burnt in the fire to their gods (Deut. 12:31). Chapter 14 of Deuteronomy lists a number of things which are an abomination to eat, including the pig, the eagle, the osprey, the vulture, the owl, the swan, the pelican, etc. (Deut. 14:3). There shall not be found among you any one that uses divination, or an observer of the times, or an enchanter, or a witch, or a charmer, or a consulter with familiar spirits, or a wizard or a necromancer; for all that do these things are an abomination unto the Lord (Deut. 18:10-12). Wearing clothes of the opposite sex was an abomination (Deut. 22:5). Money earned from prostitution cannot be given to the Lord (Deut. 23:18). A former husband taking back his wife after she was defiled was an abomination before the Lord (Deut. 24:4). Regarding sacrifices, they could not sacrifice unto the Lord a bullock or sheep that had a blemish, or foul odor; for that was an abomination unto the Lord (Deut. 17:1).

The psalmist declared there are seven abominations, a proud look, a lying tongue, hands that shed innocent blood, a heart that devises wicked imaginations, feet that be swift in running to mischief, a false witness that speaks lies and he that sows discord among brethren (Prv 6:16-19). The pretentious person has seven abominations: hatred, deceit, wickedness, ensnarement, moves boundary lines, lies and speaks flattery (Prv 26:25-28). A false balance is an abomination before the Lord (Prv 11:1); the sacrifice of the wicked is an abomination to the Lord (Prv 15:8); he that turns his ear away from hearing the law, his prayer shall be an abomination (Prv 28:9); and it is an abomination for kings to commit wickedness, because the throne is established by righteousness (Prv 16:12).

The prophets had much to say about abominations. In one of Jeremiah's first messages, he declared the Lord had brought them into a plentiful land, to eat the fruit thereof and the goodness thereof; but when they entered, they defiled his land and made his heritage an abomination (Jer. 2:7). Jeremiah speaks of how their abomination became widespread, from the least of them even unto the greatest of them, from the prophet even unto the priest, and none were ashamed when they committed abominations, neither did they blush (Jer. 6:13,15). Jeremiah prophesied the punishment of the Lord against Judah that he would recompense their iniquity and their sin double; because they have defiled his land, they have filled my inheritance with the carcasses of their detestable and abominable things (Jer. 17:18). Yet the day arrived when the Lord could no longer bear because of the evil of their abominations, therefore he made his land a desolation, an astonishment, a curse and without an inhabitant (Jer. 44:22).

Ezekiel echoed Jeremiah, adding that even the temple was defiled, and the sanctuary was defiled with their abominations. Therefore, I will also diminish you, neither shall my eye spare, neither will I have pity (Ezek 5:11). The Lord said that for all the evil abominations of the house of Israel, they will fall by the sword, by the famine and by the pestilence (Ezek 6:11). And my eye will not spare, neither will I have pity, I will recompense you according to your ways and your abominations that are in the midst of you, and you shall know that I am the Lord that smites (Ezek 7:9). The Lord called Jerusalem a harlot, because her filthiness was poured out. Her nakedness was discovered through her whoredoms with her lovers, with all the idols of her abominations and by the blood of her children. So the Lord will judge her as a woman that breaks wedlock (Ezek 16:35-38). Ezekiel charged them of bringing into the Lord's sanctuary strangers, uncircumcised in heart and uncircumcised in the flesh, to pollute it. But now when they offer bread, fat and blood, they are refused by the Lord for the covenant is broken by their abominations (Ezek 44:7). The righteous were marked by six angels that went through Jerusalem and set a mark upon the foreheads of the men that sigh and that cry against all the abominations (Ezek 9:4). Yet even the righteous, whose lives are spared, are cast out of the land with a mission to tell the heathen why they lost their land, they were spared the sword, famine and pestilence that they might declare all their abominations among the heathen (Ezek 12:16). It is the prophet Ezekiel that defines abomination so harshly. If a son is a robber, a shedder of blood, has eaten on the mountains, defiled his neighbor's wife, oppressed the poor and needy, spoiled by violence, not restored the pledge, lifted his eyes to the idols, committed abomination, given forth upon usury: he shall not live, for he has done all these abominations (Ezek 18:10-13). When the righteous turn away from their righteousness and commits iniquity, according to the abominations that the wicked, he will not live. All his righteousness that he has done will not be remembered (Ezek 18:24).

The Greek word for "abomination" is the Greek word "bdelugma" (pronounced "deugh-lou-mah"). It is found only 6 times in the NT; it is used by Jesus and the writer of Revelation.

Jesus declared of the end times that when you see the abomination of desolation, as spoken of by Daniel the prophet standing in the holy place, let him understand (Matt. 24:15). Speaking to the Pharisees, Jesus said to them that they justify themselves before others but God knows their hearts, and that which is highly esteemed among men is an abomination in the sight of God (Lk 16:15).

Regarding the woman of Revelation, she was arrayed in purple, scarlet, gold, precious stones and pearls; having a golden cup in her hand full of abominations, filthiness of her fornication. On her forehead was the name "Babylon the great", who is the mother of harlots and abominations in the earth (Rev. 17:4,5). John declared there shall, in no wise, enter into heaven anything that defiles, nor anyone who works abomination (Rev. 21:27).

In summary of the word abomination, it is something that defiles and takes away the promise of eternal life. Israel was a covenant people with Yahweh, and the covenant specified that there were sins that brought about the severe penalty of death. While serving foreign gods, the people committed abominations, such as murder and blasphemy, against the Lord. The abomination of a rebellious son who was stubborn, a glutton and a drunkard. The abomination of a child that cursed a parent. The abominations of refusal to honor the Sabbath. Also, there were the abomination of false prophets. All these OT abominations were in context of being **guilty** of rejecting the covenant. The NT uses of abomination is chiefly in context with the worship of gods or a man as a god, rather than worship of God in heaven.

Conclusion of the Unforgivable Sins:

I have chosen to categorize these four sins similar to the four personality types developed by Myers Briggs. I have applied a "character" to each of the four unforgivable sins, which I believe best suits the nature of the sin.

Apostasy began as the casual worship of the gods of other nations alongside Yahweh, but later matured into a backsliding and their walking away from the statutes of the Lord, eventually led to a repudiation of Yahweh, who called them harlots. Thus, I have chosen the "harlot" as the character of apostasy. A good example of apostasy today is the Christian taking Yoga classes.

The word "evil" speaks of cruelty, it includes slavery, murder, child sacrifice and the invention of devices to hurt others. I have chosen the "pirate" as the character to best typify evil. It is the greatest sin of all because of its disregard for human life. A good example of evil today are the Somali pirates who attack ships and hold people for hostage.

The word "wicked" has much to do with being unjust, the schemer who very subtly takes that which is not his and then, in arrogance, boasts of his theft; yet with no violence. I have chosen the "gypsy" as the character best to typify wickedness. A good example today of a wicked person is Bernie Madoff, the famous wall street ponsi schemer.

Lastly, the word "abomination" describes detestable sins like homosexuality, bestiality and other non-violent acts that defile. I have chosen the "witch" as the character to best typify abomination. Good examples today of an abominable person would be fortunetellers, tattoo artists, homosexuals and spiritualists.

The violence of the "pirate" is opposite of the more peaceful "witch or fortuneteller", whereas the craftiness of the "gypsy" is opposite of the "repudiation" of the harlot. Like the Myers-Briggs model, these are generalities only. Graphically, the words would appear like:

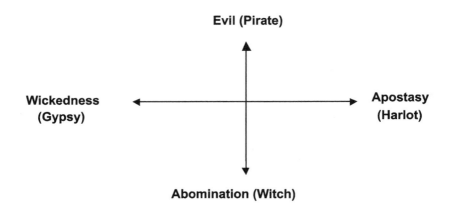

In Israel, people found **guilty** of the above four sins were separated from the congregation by means of death. In every case, the person was brought before the judges who heard the testimony of witnesses. If found **guilty**, the person was put to death. The people of Israel rarely put people to death because the judgment was not based on a single isolated incident, but by overwhelming evidence that it was a lifestyle with the person determined to live no other way.

However, there were others who were also separated from the congregation, but not by death. A man who had injury to his testicles or penis could not enter the congregation of the Lord (Deut. 23:1). Yet the man's sons had no restrictions, because it was a physical injury. Dake argues that the "congregation of the Lord" meant that the person could not come near the tabernacle/temple or hold any governmental position.[116] The descendants of a bastard or the descendants of the Ammonite and Moabite could not enter the congregation of the Lord for ten generations (Deut. 23:2,3). The descendants of the Egyptian and the Edomite could enter in the 3rd generation. Therefore, there appears to be three general groups of people, people who sinned unto death and were removed from the congregation by the death penalty, descendants of particular people groups who could not be a part of the congregation, irrespective of their sin, and those who remained in covenant by means of atoning for their sin. The Lord has always been willing to forgive, but some people's hearts are so hardened that they spurn the Lord's forgiveness to their own peril.

The NT example is very similar. The apostles witnessed many people delivered from cultic paganism into eternal salvation. Yet others spurned the gospel to their own peril.

---

116   Finis Jennings Dake, *Dake's Annotated Reference Bible*. (Lawrenceville, Georgia: Dake Bible Sales, 1963), 222.

Chapter 9

THE FORGIVABLE SINS OF IGNORANCE AND SHORTCOMING

There were four types of OT sins that were forgivable, because each sin had a corresponding sacrifice. Like unforgivable sins, these sins are a direct affront to the lordship of Yahweh and his established order by means of covenant. Unlike unforgivable sins, there is place for repentance and restitution for harm or loss, along with reintegration into the family and community. This chapter deals with the two of the four forgivable sins, because the sin of ignorance and the sin of shortcoming are direct opposite each other in nature.

1.   The Sin of Ignorance

This sin is only found 19 times in OT scripture. In the phrase, "atonement for the error which he committed unwittingly," the word for "error" is "shagag", which is pronounced "shaa-gag". Two key verses are:

"If a person sins unwittingly (shagag) he shall offer a female goat a year old for a sin offering. And the priest shall make atonement before the Lord for the person who ignorantly sins to make atonement for him; and he shall be forgiven" (Num. 15:27, 28).

"If anyone sins doing any of the things which the Lord has commanded not to be done, though he does not know it, yet he is guilty and shall bear his iniquity. He shall bring to the priest a ram without blemish out of the flock, valued by you at the price for a guilt offering, and the priest shall make atonement for him for the error (shagag) which he committed unwittingly, and he shall be forgiven. It is a guilt offering; he is guilty before the Lord" (Lev. 5:17-19).

From these verses, we obtain the concept that ignorance is no excuse for breaking the law.[117] On the great Day of Atonement, the High Priest entered the Holy of Holies for the ignorant sins of the people (Lev. 16:14). For the general population, when someone sinned ignorantly against any of the commandments of the Lord, he was to bring a young bullock without blemish unto the Lord for a sin offering (Lev. 4:2-3). For the rulers, when a ruler has sinned ignorantly against any of the commandments of the Lord, he shall bring his offering, a male kid goat without blemish (Lev. 4:22-23). If any one sins, though he does not know it is

---

117   Millard Erickson, *Christian Theology.* (Grand Rapids: Baker Books, 1983), 583.

wrong, yet he is guilty and will bear his iniquity. He will bring to the priest a ram without blemish out of the flock, valued by the priest for the price for a guilt offering, and the priest will make atonement for him for the ignorance which he committed unwittingly, and he shall be forgiven (Lev. 5:17-19). There is a specific command for the priests, for when a priest commits a trespass and sins through ignorance in the holy things of the Lord, then he shall bring for his trespass unto the Lord a ram without blemish out of the flocks, with your estimation by shekels of silver, after the shekel of the sanctuary, for a trespass offering (Lev. 5:15). If something is committed by ignorance without the knowledge of the congregation, then all the congregation will offer one young bullock for a burnt offering (Num. 15:24).

Moses instructed Joshua that when they came over Jordan into the land of Canaan, then they were to appoint refuge cities; that the killer may flee to who killed a person in ignorance (Num. 35:11,15). If the killer kills any person ignorantly and unwittingly, the city of refuge will be his refuge from the avenger of blood, and not die by the hand of the avenger of blood until he stands before the congregation (Josh. 20:3,9).

Referring to the key verse, the LXX gives the Greek word for "shagag" as "akousios" (pronounced as "awe-cou-see-oss"). "If a person sins unwittingly (akousios) he will offer a female goat a year old for a sin offering, and the priest will make atonement before the Lord for the person who ignorantly (akousios) sins to make atonement for him; and he will be forgiven." The word "akousios" is found 22 times in OT but in the NT, it only refers once to ignorance. Paul, in his address to the Corinthians, declared he was preaching the gospel willingly and not ignorantly (1 Cor 9:17). The Greeks used the word "agnoousin" (pronounced "agg-knew-sin") to refer to being uninformed of certain events or common ignorance.

In Hebrews, the office of the high priest is described as someone who can have compassion on the ignorant (agnoousin) and on them that are out of the way, for that he himself also is compassed with infirmity. Therefore, regarding the people and for himself, he offered for sins (Heb 5:2). Here those who sinned by means of ignorance, or were led astray by others, have a measure of compassion by the high priest, for he was a man like themselves. Paul in his persecution of Christians tried to make them blaspheme (Acts 26:11), yet he did it in ignorance (agnoousin) (1 Tim. 1:13).

I believe that the concept of things done in ignorance resulted in non-penalty, was well understood in NT times, and so the NT writers gave little attention to this sin.

2.   The Sin of Shortcoming

Erickson argues that this sin is a mistake, rather than a willful, conscious chosen sin.[118] The idea here is like speeding through a playground zone, you are well aware that all drivers must slow down for playground zones but you are driving in an unfamiliar area, and inadvertently do not see the playground sign. Irrespective of whether a police officer catches you or not, and irrespective if any harm is committed, you have broken the law.

The Hebrew word for shortcoming is "chata" (pronounced as "chaugh-tay"). It is found 241 times in the OT and is most often interpreted as "sin, offend and fault". The traditional key verse is "Among all this people, there were seven hundred chosen men left-handed; every one could sling stones at an hair breadth, and not miss (chata)" (Judg. 20:16). The idea behind missing the mark is like a bull's eye target, the person is well aware of the standard and has intention of hitting the mark, but fails to do so. However, the proverb, "It is not good for a man to be without knowledge, and he who makes haste with his feet misses (chata) his way," (Prv 19:2) suggests a shortcoming. In a hurry and lack of wisdom, he proceeded down a path toward ruin. For that reason, I have chosen to assign the word "shortcoming" to the word "chata", instead of "missing the mark" or "mistake".

---

118   Millard Erickson, *Christian Theology.* (Grand Rapids: Baker Books, 1983), 586.

The first use of this word is in the narrative of Abraham and Abimelech, who took Sarah as part of a covenant not knowing she was Abraham's wife. Abimelech demanded why Abraham had offended (shortcoming) him that he had brought on himself and his kingdom a great sin (shortcoming) (Gen. 20:9). When Joseph was commanded by his master's wife to lie with her, he told her he could not do a great wickedness and sin (shortcoming) toward God (Gen. 39:9). We do not know the deeds of the baker and butler, however it was a deed that cost the baker his life, the butler and baker had offended (shortcoming) their lord the king of Egypt (Gen. 40:1). When the brothers of Joseph stood before him, he tested them by demanding that Simeon be kept in prison while the brothers returned with food back to Canaan and return with Benjamin. Reuben, who had been against hurting Joseph and not a part of his sale into slavery, told his brothers to not sin (shortcoming) against the child (Gen. 42:22). When Pharaoh made the Israelites make brick with no straw, he countered their complaint with the accusation that it was their fault (shortcoming) (Ex 5:16). After the ten plagues, Pharaoh was finally broken and called for Moses and Aaron, telling them he had sinned (shortcoming), the Lord was righteous and his people were wicked (Ex 9:27). After Moses declared the ten commandments to the children of Israel, he concluded by telling them to fear not, for God has come to prove them that his fear might before their faces, that they would not sin (shortcoming) (Ex 20:20). The

Lord instructs Israel not to covenant with the inhabitants he will drive out before them, for the Lord would drive out the inhabitants but they are not to make a covenant with them or with their gods; they are not to dwell in your land, or they will make you to sin (shortcoming) against the Lord (Ex 23:31-33). Moses instructs Aaron and the priests regarding, the initiation of the sin offering, to make the priests holy by consecrating them for seven days, offering every day a bullock for a sin (shortcoming) offering for atonement, thus cleansing the altar (Ex 29:36). After the offering for the priests, Moses instructed Aaron to offer a sin offering for the people using a goat for the sin (shortcoming) (Lev. 9:15). Moses, after discovering the golden calf, told the people they had sinned (shortcoming) a great sin (shortcoming), and now he would go up unto the Lord to make an atonement for your sin (shortcoming) (Ex 32:30). Shortcoming is further defined if anyone sins (shortcoming) when he hears a public call to testify and though he is a witness, whether he has seen it or heard about it, yet he does not speak, he will bear his iniquity (Lev. 5:1). Here the individual is not a participant in the shortcoming, but merely keeps quiet. Similarly, regarding testimony, one witness will not witness against another man for an iniquity or a sin (shortcoming), but at the mouth of two witnesses will the matter be established (Deut. 19:15). Since they could not touch the dead when someone buried a dead body, on the 8th day they came and made a sin (shortcoming) offering in order to be cleansed. They brought two turtles or two young pigeons to the priest, and the priest offered the one up for a sin (shortcoming) offering and the other for a burnt offering (Num. 6:10-11). When Miriam and Aaron murmured, Miriam became leprous and Aaron told Moses to not lay the sin (shortcoming) upon them, because they had both done foolishly and sinned (shortcoming) (Num. 12:11). After the rebellion of Korah against the leadership of Moses, Moses and Aaron cried to the God of all flesh, begging if one man sins (shortcoming) would God be angry with all the people (Num. 16:22)? After King Arad of the Canaanites came against Israel and the Lord gave Israel a great victory at Hormah, yet the children complained. The Lord sent serpents among them, killing many, so the people came to Moses and confessed they had sinned (shortcoming), for they had spoken against the Lord and against Moses (Num. 21:7). When the spies came back with fear of the giants, Moses told them that only Joshua and Caleb would enter the Promised Land, and the people confessed their fear as sin (shortcoming) (Deut. 1:41).

Samuel said to the people of Israel that as for him, God forbid that he should sin (shortcoming) before the Lord in ceasing to pray for them, but that he would teach them the good and right way (1 Sam. 12:23). It was reported to King Saul that after the defeat of the Philistines, the people of Israel killed sheep and oxen, and sinned (shortcoming) against the Lord in that they ate the blood with the meat

(1 Sam. 14:33, 34). King Saul confessed before Samuel he had sinned (shortcoming), for he had transgressed the commandment of the Lord because he feared the people (1 Sam. 15:24). Jonathan spoke to his father King Saul about David telling the king not to sin (shortcoming) against David, because David had not sinned (shortcoming) against him (1 Sam. 19:4). After David spared King Saul's life, Saul declared he had sinned (shortcoming), promising no more harm to David (1 Sam. 26:21). After David repents for his involvement with Bathsheba, he is rebuked by the prophet Nathan and David confessed to Nathan he had sinned (shortcoming) against the Lord. Then Nathan told David the Lord had put away his sin (shortcoming) and he would not die (2 Sam. 12:13).

When King Jeroboam set up a false altar at Bethel and created a false priesthood, the prophet Ahijah prophesied that the Lord would smite Israel and give up Israel because of the sins (shortcomings) of Jeroboam, who made Israel to sin (shortcoming) (1 Kgs 14:16). King Hezekiah's son, Manasseh, is called the most evil king of Israel by the Lord, because Manasseh did abominations and evil above all that the Amorites did, and made Judah also to sin (shortcoming) with his idols (2 Kgs 21:11). His actions apparently were both evil and abominable because he had no excuse, whereas participation by the people was deemed by the Lord a lighter matter probably because they were commanded by the king to participate.

Isaiah said the Lord gave Jacob for a spoil, and Israel he turned over to, because they had sinned (shortcoming), not walking in his ways nor obedient to his law (Isa. 42:24).

Jeremiah complained to King Jedekiah, demanding he answer what offence (shortcoming) he had done against the king, his servants or his people that landed him in prison (Jer. 37:18). Jeremiah prophesied against Babylon that the Lord would take vengeance with armies in array all around her, they were to bend the bow and shoot, sparing no arrows because Babylon had sinned (shortcoming) against the Lord (Jer. 50:14).

Ezekiel taught that if you warn the righteous man so the righteous man does not sin (shortcoming), and he does not sin (shortcoming), then he will live (Ezek 3:21). The Lord tells Ezekiel that when the land sins (shortcoming) against him by trespassing grievously, then he will stretch out his hand upon it and break the staff of the bread with famine (Ezek 14:13).

The Greek word translated for the Hebrew word "chata" is the word "amartia" (pronounced "haa-mart-tea-awh"). It occurs 173 times in the NT, most commonly as "sin".[119]

The angel said to Joseph that Mary will bring forth a son and he would call him Jesus; for he will save his people from their sins (shortcomings) (Matt. 1:21). Note, it does not say Jesus will save his people from all sin. Zacharias

---

119   Frederick William Danker, *A Greek-English Lexicon.* (Chicago: University of Chicago Press, 2000), 50.

prophesied about his son John, declaring his son would be called the prophet of the Highest, for he will go before the face of the Lord to prepare his ways and give knowledge of salvation unto his people for the remission of their sins (shortcomings) (Lk 1:77). John the Baptist baptized the people in the Jordan River as they confessed their sins (shortcomings) (Matt. 3:6). John said, "Behold the Lamb of God, which takes away the sin (shortcomings) of the world" (Jn 1:29). Jesus said to the sick of the palsy, "Son, be of good cheer, your sins (shortcomings) are forgiven" (Matt. 9:2). That was something only the priests could do, and angered the Pharisees. When Jesus was eating in the house of a Pharisee, a woman came to him, opened an alabaster box of perfume and washed his feet with her tears and wiped them with her hair. Jesus declared her sins (shortcomings), which are many, were forgiven (Lk 7:47). When the blind man was healed by Jesus, the Pharisees told the man he was born in sin (shortcomings) so he had nothing to say to them (Jn 9:34). Jesus responded to the Pharisees by declaring if they were blind, they would have no sin (short-coming); but because they said they could see, their sin (shortcoming) remained (Jn 9:41). When the Pharisees began to say Jesus cast out devils by Beelzebub, Jesus said that all manner of sin (shortcomings) and blasphemy will be forgiven unto men, but the blasphemy against the Holy Ghost will not be forgiven (Matt. 12:31). Jesus told the Pharisees that he was about to go, but that they would seek him and will die in their sins (shortcomings) because where he was going they could not go (Jn 8:21). Jesus then told the Pharisees that whoever commits sin (shortcoming) is the servant of sin (shortcoming) (Jn 8:34). When the disciples asked Jesus to teach them to pray, Jesus ended the prayer with, "And forgive us our sins (shortcomings), for we also forgive everyone that is indebted to us, and lead us not into temptation, but deliver us from evil" (Lk 11:4). This asks the question, are Christians required to forgive evil? At the Lord's Supper, Jesus took the cup and said, "For this is the blood of the new testament, which is shed for you for the remission of sins (shortcomings)" (Matt. 26:29). This asks the question, does the blood of Christ forgive evil?

Luke declares the great commission, that repentance and remission of sins (shortcomings) should be preached in his name among all nations, beginning at Jerusalem (Lk 24:47). Jesus told Pilate he had no power against him, except it was given him from above; therefore, he that delivered me unto you has the greater sin (shortcoming) (Jn 19:11). Jesus, speaking of the Holy Ghost, said that when he is come, he will reprove the world of sin (shortcoming), of righteousness and of judgment. Of sin (shortcoming), because they believed not on him; of righteousness, because he went to his father; and of judgment, because the prince of this world is judged (Jn 16:8-11). Jesus breathed on the disciples to receive the Holy Ghost that whose sins shortcomings they remit, they are remitted; whose sins (shortcoming) they retain, they are retained (Jn 20:23). Do pastors only have the authority to forgive shortcomings and not evil?

Peter told to the crowd to repent and be baptized, each one of them, in the name of Jesus Christ for the remission of sins (shortcoming), and they would receive the gift of the Holy Ghost (Acts 2:38). Peter also preached that they were to be converted that their sins (shortcoming) may be blotted out, when the times of refreshing will come from the presence of the Lord (Acts 3:19). This asks the question; "Can evil be blotted out?" Peter preached to Cornelius that Christ gave all the prophets witness that through his name, whoever believes in him will receive remission of sins (shortcomings) (Acts 10:43).

Paul recounts his Damascus road experience when Jesus told him he was sending him to open their eyes from darkness to light, and from the power of Satan to God; that they might receive forgiveness of sins (shortcoming) (Acts 26:18). Paul also declared to the Romans that they had proven both Jew and Gentiles are all under sin (shortcoming) (Rom 3:9). By one man, sin (shortcoming) entered into the world, and death by sin (shortcoming) so death passed upon all men for that all have sinned (shortcoming), for until the law sin (shortcoming) was in the world, but sin (shortcoming) is not imputed when there is no law (Rom 8:12-13). For by the deeds of the law, no flesh will be justified in his sight, for by the law is the knowledge of sin (shortcoming) (Rom 3:20). For what the law could not do in that it was weak through the flesh, God sent his own son in the likeness of sinful (shortcoming) flesh and for sin (shortcoming) condemned sin (shortcoming) in the flesh (Rom 8:3). Should you continue in sin (shortcoming) that grace might abound? God forbid. How can we that are dead to sin (shortcoming) live any longer in them (Rom 6:1- 2)? For whatever is not of faith is sin (shortcoming) (Rom 14:23). The sting of death is sin (shortcoming), and the strength of sin (shortcoming) is the law (1 Cor 15:55). But the Lord made him to be sin (shortcoming) for us, who knew no sin (shortcoming), that we might be the righteousness of God in him (2 Cor 5:21). You hath he quickened who were dead in trespasses and sins (shortcoming) (Eph 2:1).

The writer of Hebrews declares that Christ, by the brightness of his glory and the express image of his person, and upholding all things by the word of his power, when he had by himself purged our sins (shortcomings), sat down on the right hand of the Majesty on High (Heb 1:3). Therefore, in all things, our faithful high priest in things pertaining to God makes reconciliation for the sins (shortcoming) of the people (Heb 2:17). Christ, as High Priest, did what Aaron could not do, for it is not possible that the blood of bulls and goats could take away sins (shortcoming) (Heb 10:4). This begs the question, if Christ therefore takes away sins once covered by sacrifice, what about sins not covered by sacrifice? Christ was once offered to bear the sins (shortcoming) of many, and to them that look for him shall he appear the second time without sin (shortcoming) unto salvation (Heb 9:28). The writer of Hebrews ends with an exhortation to uplift one another daily so that none of you be hardened through the deceitfulness of sin (shortcoming) (Heb 3:13).

James instructs that he that knows to do good and does it not, to him it is sin (shortcoming) (Jas 4:17). If any man sees his brother sin (shortcoming), a sin (shortcoming) which is not unto death, he shall ask and he shall be given him life for them that sin (shortcoming) not unto death. There is a sin (shortcoming) unto death. All unrighteousness is sin (shortcoming), but there is a sin (shortcoming) unto death (1 Jn 5:16,17). James very clearly distinguishes between shortcomings and a sin unto death, that is a shortcoming that had provision of forgiveness that grew to a point of being evil. We all learn to sin because in it is an inherited nature, but if we are not careful to repent of sins as long as they remain forgivable, they have the potential of igniting such hatred that violent acts erupt, causing the person to commit unforgivable sin. All of us are **guilty** of shortcomings in life, may we learn to repent quickly.

Chapter 10

THE FORGIVABLE SINS OF REBELLION AND PERVERSION

The sins of rebellion and iniquity often go hand-in-hand, for when truth is twisted, it leads to iniquity and when iniquity abounds, it often matures into rebellion.

1. The sin of Rebellion

The sin of rebellion is expressed with the word "pesha" (pronounced "pea-shaw"). This word occurs 135 times on the OT and is the sin of Adam, it was often used to describe the rebellion of subjected nations, used to describe the rebellion between two parties and used by the prophets as a description of the forceful rejection of the law.

Regarding the sin of Adam and Eve, this word describes the first sin. Job is the only person in the OT that mentions Adam's sin, who said if he covered his transgressions (rebellion) like Adam did, by hiding his iniquity in his bosom, then let thistles grow on his land instead of wheat (Job 31:33).

There are three key verses for this word regarding vassal nations. The second book of Kings opens with, "Then Moab rebelled (pesha) against Israel after the death of Ahab." Mesha, king of Moab, was a sheep master and rendered unto the king of Israel a hundred thousand lambs and a hundred thousand rams yearly; but when Ahab was dead, the king of Moab rebelled against Israel (2 Kgs 3:4-5). This was significant annual tribute. King Jehoram, the son of Ahab, now aligns himself with King Jehoshaphat of Judah and, with the instruction of Elisha, they obtain a significant victory over Moab. Later when Jehoram, son of Jehoshaphat, came to rule, the Edomites rebelled (pesha) (2 Kgs 8:20). This rebellion is the throwing off of a conquering nation by revoking the vassal agreement.

Moses instituted a law, if when two men came at odds against each other regarding ownership of something:

> "For all manner of trespass (pesha), whether it be for ox, for ass, for sheep, for raiment, or for any manner of lost thing, which another challenges to be his, the cause of both parties shall come before the judges; and who the judges shall condemn, he shall pay double unto his neighbor" (Ex 22:9).

Thus under Mosaic Law, the idea that "finders keepers, loser's weepers" has no validity but rather the person found **guilty** had to repay double to the neighbor. The KJV renders this verse as "all manner of trespass", but the "trespass offering" uses a different word; "And he shall bring his trespass (asham) offering unto the Lord for his sin (chata) which he hath sinned (chata) (Lev. 5:6). The word "asham" means offense, rather than trespass. However, the best-known verse for this sin is, "As far as the east is from the west, so far has he removed our transgressions (pesha) from us" (Ps 103:13).

Regarding the patriarchs, Jacob was angry with Laban and demanded Laban answer what was his trespass (rebellion) and what was his sin (shortcoming) that he have so hotly pursued after him (Gen. 31:36). The last words of Jacob were to be passed along to Joseph that he forgive the trespass (rebellion) of his brothers and their sin (shortcoming), for they did unto him evil and also forgive the trespass (rebellion) of the servants of the God of your father (Gen. 50:17). In fulfillment of patriarchal and Mosaic prophecies, the tribes of Joseph's two sons, Ephraim and Manasseh, received a double portion of land when Israel entered the Promised Land, because of the actions of the brothers.[120]

The High Priest made atonement for the holy place because of the uncleanness of the children of Israel, and because of their transgressions (rebellion) in all their sins (shortcoming). Likewise he did for the tabernacle of the congregation that remained among them in the midst of

---

120   Maureen Gaglardi, *The Path of the Just*, Vol. 2, (Vancouver: New West Press, 1971), 297.

their uncleanness (Lev. 16:16). Joshua told the people they could not serve the Lord, for he is a holy God; he is a jealous God; he will not forgive their transgressions (rebellion) or their sins (shortcoming) if they forsake the Lord, and serve strange gods. Then he will turn and do them hurt, and consume you after he has done them good (Josh. 24:19, 20).

David shouted to Saul that he was not **guilty** of rebellion, as he held up the skirt of Saul's robe in his hand that he cut off but did not kill him. David did not have evil, transgression (rebellion), or had he sinned (shortcoming) against Saul, yet Saul hunted David's soul (1 Sam. 24:11). Solomon prays at the dedication of the temple a prayer for the Lord's compassion that if they rebel and are carried away, the Lord forgive his people who have rebelled against him, and all their rebelling which they have committed against the Lord; and grant them compassion in the sight of those who will carry them away captive (1 Kgs 8:50). When the kingdom was about to be divided, Solomon's son Rehoboam sent Adoram to all the tribes to collect taxes. But the ten tribes rebelled by killing Adoram, rejecting the reign of Rehoboam over the ten tribes of Israel, and so Israel has rebelled against the house of David to this day (1 Kgs 12:19).

Ezra instructed the men of Israel to divorce their foreign wives so that the Lord can send rain if they obey; but there were many who have transgressed (rebelled) in this thing (Ezr 10:13). Those men were forced to leave the country.

Elihu falsely accused Job of rebellion, declaring his desire was that Job be tried to the end because of his answers for wicked men. Elihu said Job added rebellion to his sin (shortcoming) and then clapped his hands and multiplied his words against God (Job 34:36-37). The psalmist declared, "Then will I teach transgressors (rebels) your ways, and sinners (shortcoming) will be converted onto you" (Ps 51:13). A brother offended (rebelled against) is harder to be won than a strong city (Prv 18:19).

Isaiah declared the Lord has nourished and brought up children, but they have rebelled against me, the ox and the ass know their master, but Israel does not know me (Isa. 1:2). Isaiah spoke of the end times to come, declaring that there will be earthquakes upon the land to remove the weight of rebellion, the earth will reel back and forth like a drunkard and will be removed like a cottage. Because the transgression (rebellion) is heavy upon it, it will fall and not rise again (Isa. 20:19). Again, Isaiah told Israel that they had never heard, they had never known, from of old their ear has not been opened; for the Lord knew that they would deal very faithlessly, and from birth they were called a rebel (Isa. 48:8). Isaiah speaking of the Messiah, declared the Lord would divide him a portion with the great, he will divide the spoil with the strong; because he poured out his soul to death. He was numbered with the transgressors (rebels); yet he bore the sin (shortcoming) of many and made intercession for the transgressors (rebels) (Isa. 53:12). Probably the most interesting use of the word "rebellion" is found in Isaiah, where Isaiah concludes his writing with a description of hell, "And they shall go forth and look on the dead bodies of the men that have rebelled against me; for their worm shall not die, their fire shall not be quenched, and they shall be an abhorrence to all flesh" (Isa. 66:24).

Jeremiah brings an accusation against the priests, pastors and prophets, for the priests no longer inquired as to where the Lord is. The priests who handle the law do not know the Lord, the shepherds rebelled against me and the prophets prophesied by Baal (Jer. 2:8). The word of the Lord came to Jeremiah in prison that the coming destruction of Jerusalem was for the purpose of purification, with the promise that the Lord will cleanse them from all their iniquity. Though they sinned (shortcoming) against him, he will pardon all their iniquities, whereby they had sinned (shortcoming) and whereby they had transgressed (rebelled) against him (Jer. 33:8).

The Lord sent Ezekiel to the people of Israel, a nation of rebels, who had rebelled against the Lord just like their fathers rebelled (Ezek 2:3). That the house of Israel may go no more astray from the Lord, neither be polluted any more with their transgressions (rebellion) and the Lord may be their God (Ezek 14:11). Ezekiel gives instructions to the captives to cast away all their transgressions (rebellion), whereby they have transgressed (rebelled), and make themselves a new heart and a new spirit, for there is no reason for them to die (Ezek 18:31).

Daniel prophetically speaks of seventy weeks Israel must go through to be cleansed. For seventy weeks are determined upon your people and upon your holy city: to finish the transgression (rebellion), to make an end of sins (shortcoming), to make reconciliation for iniquity, to bring everlasting righteousness, to seal up the vision and prophesy, and to anoint the most Holy (Dan. 9:24). Daniel clearly specifies the three chief sins of Israel are rebellion, shortcoming and iniquity.

Hosea speaks about God's desire to heal Israel, but they would not turn from rebelling, but instead they have fled from the Lord, destruction came to them because they had transgressed (rebelled), though the Lord had redeemed them, yet they have spoken lies against the Lord (Hos. 7:13). Set the trumpet to your mouth, for he will come as an eagle against the house of the Lord, because they have transgressed my covenant and trespassed (rebelled) against my law (Hos. 8:1). Here, the word for transgressed is "abar", which means "to cause to pass away" like "taking away a garment".[121] A better translation would be, "They caused my covenant to pass away and rebelled against my law." Hosea concludes his writing with a warning; the wise

---

121   F. Brown, S. Driver, C. Briggs, *The Brown-Driver-Briggs Hebrew and English Lexicon.* (Peabody, Mass.: Hendrickson, 2003), 719.

will understand these things, for the ways of the Lord are right and the just will walk in them, but the transgressor (rebel) will fall (Hos. 14:9).

The Lord mocks the false priests and false temple at Bethel on Mount Gilgal where Israel worshipped, inviting them to come to Bethel and transgress (rebel). At Gilgal, they multiply transgressions (rebellion) so they are to bring their sacrifices every morning, but your tithes only every three years (Amos 4:4). Zephaniah declared that one day Israel will no longer be ashamed for all their doings by which they transgressed (rebelled) against the Lord, for the Lord will take out of the midst of them those that rejoice in their pride, and they will no longer be haughty because of my holy mountain (Zeph 3:11).

In the NT, the sin of rebellion is expressed by the word "atheteo" (pronounced "awe-thee-tea-owe"), which occurs 64 times in the LXX and 16 times in the NT. Danker argues that this word means, "to reject something, to invalidate something, to set aside as worthless, or to go back on your word."[122] Referring to the key verse, the LXX uses the word "atheteo" for the word rebellion, "Then Moab rebelled (atheteo) against Israel after the death of Ahab."

The daughter of Herodias, with haste, asked Herod for the head of John the Baptist, and though Herod was greatly

---

122   Frederick William Danker, *A Greek-English Lexicon*. (Chicago: University of Chicago Press, 2000), 24.

sorrowful, yet for his oath's sake, he did not refuse (atheteo) her (Mk 6:27). Jesus, speaking about the Pharisees, quoted Isaiah, declaring that in vain they worship by teaching commandments of men but reject (rebellion) the commandments of God, that they could keep their own traditions (Mk 7:9). This is repeated by Luke, who wrote the Pharisees, and lawyers rejected (rebelled) the counsel of God against themselves by not willing to be baptized of him (Lk 7:30). Jesus declared to his disciples that whoever hears them hears him, but he that despises (rebellion) them despises (rebellion) him; and he that despises (rebellion) him, despises (rebellion) he that sent him (Lk 10:17). In a similar fashion, John wrote that he that rejects (rebellion) me (Jesus), and receives not his words, has one that judges him, the word that he has spoken, the same will judge him in the last day (Jn 12:48).

Paul compared the covenants of men to the covenant of Christ, once confirmed no man can disannul (rebellion) or add to it (Gal 3:15). Paul instructs the Thessalonians that God had not called them to uncleanness, but to holiness, because he that despises (rebellion) despises (rebellion) not man, but God, who also had given them the Holy Ghost (1 Thes 4:7-8).

The writer of Hebrews reminded his readers that anyone that despised (rebelled) the law of Moses died without mercy under two or three witnesses (Heb 10:28). Jude wrote that those who defiled the flesh despised (rebellion) dominion, and spoke evil of dignities will suffer eternal fire (Jude 1:7-8).

In summary, the concept behind rebellion is a rejection of the system, not mere "I want to do it my way" concept of trespassing. It is someone who is **guilty** of totally rejecting all law, a rejection of all that is holy or pure, even to the point of ridicule.

2.   The sin of Perversion

The Hebrew word for iniquity "awon" (pronounced as "awe-vone"). This sin is mentioned 233 times in the OT and comes from the root word "awah", which means, "to twist, to pervert, to bend, to distort" and is most commonly translated as the word "iniquity".[123] What is sinister about this sin is that it is often very subtle, but becomes generational very quickly, the children trusting their parents have taught them correctly, believing the perversion as truth. The Lord sends his prophets to correct the perversion, because the perversion grows gradually until God must answer with wrath to destroy it.

Job considered the faithfulness of God in the midst of adversity, declaring that God looks upon men, and if anyone confesses they have sinned (shortcoming) and perverted (iniquity) that which was right, and it profited them not, he

---

123   F. Brown, S. Driver, C. Briggs, *The Brown-Driver-Briggs Hebrew and English Lexicon.* (Peabody, Mass.: Hendrickson, 2003), 730.

will deliver his soul from going to the pit and his life will see the light (Job 33:27-28).

Jeremiah declared that upon the high places there was weeping and supplications for the children of Israel, because for they had perverted (iniquity) their way and they had forgotten the Lord (Jer. 3:21).

The reason why the sin of perversion (or iniquity) belongs to the group of sacrificial sins is that on the Day of Atonement, the High Priest took two almost identical goats and by casting lots, one goat was selected as the sin (shortcoming) and the other as the scapegoat. Leviticus records how Aaron laid both his hands upon the head of the scapegoat and confessed over the scapegoat all the iniquities (perversions) of the children of Israel, all their transgressions (rebellions) and all their sins (shortcomings), putting them on the head of the scapegoat. Then, the goat was set free into the wilderness, bearing upon it all their iniquities (perversions) in a land not inhabited (Lev. 16:21-22).

This sin is first mentioned with Cain, who tried to substitute a false sacrifice. Cain said to the Lord his punishment (perversion) was greater than he could bear (Gen. 4:13). The KJV says, "My punishment is greater than I can bear," however, Adam Clarke argues this phrase is more accurately translated, "Is my crime too great to be forgiven?" Clarke says the word "avon" can be translated punishment or crime according to context.[124] I would argue that the cause of the problem was a perversion of the required sacrifice. Though the NT scriptural references to Cain paint him as an evil man, it does so at the time of the murder, and this plea shows the possibility that Cain later indeed obtained forgiveness. The mark he received prevented anyone from killing him, giving him time to bear his judgment and come to repentance. Clement, a disciple of Peter and, afterwards, the bishop of Rome, wrote in his book, "The First Epistle of Clement to the Corinthians" that it was envy and emulation which was the source of all strife and disorder that caused Cain to kill his brother, Abel. Therefore, Clement believed that it was a long-standing feud, but nothing in scripture supports such a conclusion.

When the Lord appeared to Abram, he promised him long life and that his seed would serve in a strange land for four hundred years; but in the fourth generation they will come back, for the iniquity (perversion) of the Amorites was not yet full (Gen. 15:15-16). Before the destruction of Sodom, the angels instructed Lot to take his wife and two daughters; otherwise, they would be consumed in the iniquity (perversion) of the city (Gen. 19:15). Joseph put his silver cup in Benjamin's sack and sent his ten brothers toward home, only to have his own troops catch up to the brothers and discover the cup in Benjamin's sack. Judah

124   Adam Clarke, *Clarke's Commentary*, vol 1, (Nashville: Abingdon Press, 1836), 60.

confesses that Yahweh had found out their iniquity (perversion) because "Joseph was killed", which was a perversion of "Joseph was sold" (Gen. 44:16). Job supplies the final example of iniquity before the law was given. Job gives a somber definition of iniquity, declaring that since he had made a covenant with his eyes never to look upon a virgin, a heinous crime, an iniquity (perversion) to be punished by the judges. For this perversion was a fire that would consume all he owned if he were **guilty** (Job 32:1,11-12).

Concerning the first commandment, the Lord told Israel he was a jealous God, visiting the iniquity (perversion) of the fathers upon the children unto the third and fourth generation (Ex 20:5). This is repeated later as Yahweh declares he keeps mercy for thousands, forgiving iniquity (perversion), transgression and sin. But by no means will Yahweh clear the **guilty**, for he will visit the iniquity (perversions) of the fathers upon the children, and upon the children's children, unto the third and to the fourth generation (Ex 34:7).

Moses instructed the making of the plate of pure gold, which was engraved "Holiness to the Lord" and was worn as the High Priest headdress, that Aaron might bear the iniquity (perversion) of the holy things and gifts (Ex 28:38). The idea here is that if the gift or utensil used as part of the ceremony became a custom or common instead of holy, that the perversion or disrespect of that which is holy be forgiven. This is followed by a promise that if a soul sins by hearing the voice of swearing and is a witness, if he does not speak up, then he shall be part of the iniquity (perversion) (Lev. 5:1). Moses instructed the peace offering to be eaten within two days, with the remainder burnt totally with fire. If any of the flesh of the sacrifice of the peace offerings is eaten on the third day, the offering will not be accepted, his sin will not be forgiven and he will bear his iniquity (perversion) (Lev. 7:18). Regarding the spirit of jealousy, if a woman secretly had an affair and her husband suspects her, the husband will present an offering of jealousy, which will bring iniquity (perversion) to be revealed (Num. 5:15). If, in fact, the woman is **guilty**, then the husband will be guiltless from iniquity (perversion): but the wife will bear her iniquity (perversion) (Num. 5:31). Concerning making vows, if a man makes a vow it will stand before the Lord, but if his daughter or wife makes a vow and if the same day the man hears of it, he may disallow the vow of his daughter or wife and it will not stand. However, if he fails to disallow the vow, then he will bear her iniquity (perversion) because he permitted it (Num. 30:15).

The Lord holds his ministers to a higher standard, as seen in the life of Eli, for his sons had sex with women who came to offer their gifts on the altar. For that reason, the Lord has sworn to the house of Eli that the iniquity (perversion) of Eli's house will not be purged with sacrifice nor offering forever (1 Sam. 3:14). When king Saul spoke to the witch at En-dor, he promised her that there would be no iniquity (perversion) happen to her for her help (1 Sam. 28:19), even though it was a lie. He had no authority to act as priest and cleanse iniquity for a woman with a familiar spirit; witchcraft was punishable by death. After Saul's death, Abner, the general over Saul's army, made Saul's son Ishbosheth, king over the ten tribes. But when Ishbosheth accused Abner of going into his father's concubine, Abner protested that after he had shown kindness to the house of Saul, that he was charged with iniquity (perversion) concerning the concubine (2 Sam. 3:8). He was so enraged he went over to David's army. After David carried out a census against the command of the Lord, he repented, confessing his sin (shortcoming) and beseeched the Lord to take away his iniquity (perversion), for he had acted foolishly (2 Sam. 24:10).

After the widow at Zarephath had provided for Elijah, her son fell sick and died. She knew her worship of the Lord was after the manner of Jeroboam, so she accused Elijah of remembering her iniquity (perversion) as reason the Lord killed her son (1 Kgs 17:18).

The best-known Psalm about iniquity is, "Behold I was shaped in iniquity (perversion) and in sin (shortcoming) did my mother conceive me" (Ps 51:5). Yahweh warns Israel that if they break his statutes and do not keep his commandments, then he will visit their transgression (rebellion) with a rod and their iniquity (perversions) with stripes (Ps 89:32). This asks the question, "If Christ bore our transgressions and iniquity by his stripes, what of greater sins like evil or wickedness?"

171

When Isaiah saw the Lord high and lifted up, he cried in despair, but a seraphim took a live coal from off the altar and he laid it on his mouth, declaring his iniquity (perversion) was taken away and his sin (shortcoming) purged (Isa. 6:7). The Lord said he would punish the world for their evil, the wicked for their iniquities (perversions) and the proud would cease (Isa. 13:11). For the judgment over Judah, the Lord declared that for the iniquity (perversions) of Jacob to be purged, the fruit of taking away his sin (shortcoming) is the beating asunder all the chalkstone incense altars and groves of Asherah (Isa. 27:9). The Lord had been wearied by the iniquities (perversions) of the children of Israel (Isa. 43:24). Yet Yahweh still promised that the coming kingdom for Israel promises Jerusalem to be a quiet habitation, where no one will say they are sick because the people will be forgiven their iniquity (perversions) (Isa. 33:24). Prophetically speaking of the Messiah, Isaiah declared he was wounded for our transgressions, he was bruised for our iniquities (perversions), the chastisement of our peace was upon him and with his stripes we are healed (Isa. 53:5). Isaiah tells Israel that their iniquities (perversions) have separated them from their God, their sins (shortcomings) had hid his face from them and the Lord will not hear them (Isa. 59:2). Isaiah declared idolatry as a core reason of iniquity for their iniquities (perversions) and the iniquities (perversions) of their fathers who have burned incense on the mountains and blasphemed his name on the hills: therefore, the Lord will measure their former works into the bosom of their descendants who were alive (Isa. 65:7).

Jeremiah witnesses the perversion of idolatry, claiming Israel had turned back to the iniquities (perversions) of their forefathers, who had refused to hear of the Lord but went after other gods and had broken his covenant (Jer. 11:10). Jeremiah makes a clear distinction between perversion and shortcoming. He prophesied that when they are forced from their land, they will come asking what was their iniquity (perversion) or what was their sin (shortcoming) that they had committed against the Lord (Jer. 16:10). Jeremiah cries to the Lord, regarding his enemies, that the Lord not forgive their iniquities (perversions) or blot out their sins (short-comings) from your sight (Jer. 18:23). Ezekiel, speaking of Lucifer, writes that Lucifer was perfect in his ways from the day that he was created till iniquity (perversion) was found in him (Ezek 28:15).

The Hebrew word "awon" is the Greek word "anomia" (pronounced "aw-know-me-aye"). The word occurs 15 times in the NT.

Jesus warned about false teachers by declaring he will say to them that he never knew them, depart from him they that work iniquity (perversion) (Matt. 7:23). After the Parable of the Tares, Jesus prophesied about the end times, that the son of man will send his angels to gather out of his kingdom all things that offend and they which do iniquity (perversion) (Matt. 13:41). The word for "offend" is the word "skandala", which means, "cause to sin, cause to be brought to a downfall, entice, to trap."[125] It comes into the English language as "scandalous", and the trigger of a trap is a "scandelon". Therefore, those who belong to the kingdom but bring either scandal or perversion are removed. Jesus condemns the Scribes and Pharisees with the words, "Even so you appear righteous unto men, but within you are full of hypocrisy (upokriseos) and iniquity" (perversion) (Matt. 23:28). The word "upokriseos" means, "pretense, creating a public appearance in odds with one's real intent, insincere, smooth talker, hypocrite."[126] The Greek word for "Pharisees" is "Pharisaioi" which means, "separated ones".[127] Though the party had played an important role in the time of Maccabees, separating the role of king and priest, by the time of Christ's ministry they pre-dominately were concerned about separating people from sin. Therefore, they were endlessly adding rules upon rules to keep the people on what they believed was the straight and narrow, but Jesus recognized their rules as perversion. That is why Jesus finishes his condemnation with, "How can you escape the damnation of hell?" Jesus in the Olivet discourse prophesied that many false prophets will rise and

---

125   Frederick William Danker, *A Greek-English Lexicon*. (Chicago: University of Chicago Press, 2000), 926.

126   Frederick William Danker, *A Greek-English Lexicon*. (Chicago: University of Chicago Press, 2000),1038.

127   Ibid, Danker, 1049.

will deceive many, because iniquity (perversion) will abound, and the love of many will wax cold (Matt. 24:11-12).

In Peter's first sermon, he preached that Jesus was delivered by the determinate counsel and foreknowledge of God, but that he had taken by wicked (perverted) hands which crucified him (Acts 2:23).

Paul, speaking of justification by faith, quoted the life of as one who was blessed, because his iniquities (perversions) were forgiven and his sins (shortcomings) were covered (Rom 4:7). The promise is that iniquity (perversion) can be forgiven but it is in the context of David, a man who earnestly sought after the forgiveness with much travail. Paul addressing the Romans declared that he spoke after the manner of men, because of the infirmity of their flesh, for they had yielded their members as servants to uncleanness (akatharsia) and to iniquity (perversion) upon iniquity (perversion); but now are they to yield their members as servants to righteousness unto holiness (Rom 6:19). The word "akatharsia" means, "moral decay, vile sexual behavior, filthy behavior".[128] Rome was famous for its cultic fornication and its consequential light esteem of marriage contracts, for the Roman government had encouraged the practice of concubines and the gift of the use of

---

128   Frederick William Danker, *A Greek-English Lexicon*. (Chicago: University of Chicago Press, 2000), 34.

concubines as an act of friendship between Roman men.[129] Paul exhorts the new believers to chase after holiness with as much energy as they had chased after every vile sexual act. Paul urged the Corinthians to not be unequally yoked together with unbelievers for what fellowship has righteousness with unrighteousness (perversion); and what communion has light with darkness (2 Cor 6:14)? Though in English righteousness is contrasted with unrighteousness, Paul contrasts the rightness of justice with perversion. Paul, speaking of the end times, told the Thessalonians that they are to let no one deceive them by any means; for that day will not come except there be a falling away first, and that man of sin (perversion) be revealed, the son of perdition (apoleias) (2 Thes 2:3). The word "apoleias" means "annihilation, absolute destruction".[130] The man to be revealed in the end time will have two qualifications, his ability to pervert and his ability to utterly destroy. Paul, on the same subject, declared the fate of Satan, that wicked (perverted) one will be revealed who the Lord will consume with the spirit of his mouth, and will destroy with the brightness of his coming (2 Thes 2:8). Paul writing to Timothy speaks of Christ, who gave himself for us, that he might redeem us

---

129   Aline Rouselle, *Porneia: On Desire and the Body in Antiquity.* (Oxford: Basel Blackwell Inc., 1988), 97.

130   Ibid, Danker, 127.

from iniquity (perversion) and purify unto himself a peculiar people, zealous of good works (Ti 2:14).

The writer of Hebrews declared of Christ his throne is forever, a scepter of righteousness is the scepter of his kingdom, because he loved righteousness and hated iniquity (perversion), therefore God anointed him with the oil of gladness (Heb 1:8,9). The writer of Hebrews also speaks of the people of Israel in the last days that the covenant he will make with them in those days by putting his laws into their hearts, and into their minds, their sins (shortcomings) and iniquities (perversions) will he remember no more (Heb 10:17).

The Apostle John declares we are the sons of God but adds a warning about sin, for whoever commits sin (shortcoming) transgresses (perverts) also the law.

> "For sin (shortcoming) is the transgression (perversion) of the law, and know that he was manifested to take away our sins (shortcomings), and in him is no sin (shortcoming). Whosoever abides in him, sins (shortcomings) not, whosoever sins (shortcomings) has not seen him, neither knows him" (1 Jn 3:4-6).

The phrase, "whoever commits sin transgresses also the law. For sin is the transgression of the law," is a poor translation. The word "law" does not exist in the verse, and there is a conjunction "and" between sin and transgresses.

A better translation would be, "All who make sin and make transgressions, and the sin becomes iniquity", or better English, "Whoever commits sins or transgressions because sin becomes iniquity." The word for "sin" in the phrase, "whosoever sins has not seen him" is an active participle verb meaning a continuous action. Therefore, it is the active shortcoming that leads to perversion.

Gruits argues that iniquity is a weakness, in a particular area of our nature, that is born in us as a result of the sins of our forefathers.[131] Gruits also says that iniquity is born in us through our parents, a weakness in us that is the breeding ground for sin and in this area, Satan tempts us to transgress against God's laws.[132] Though Gruits rightly identifies the generational tendency of iniquity, she fails to identify iniquity as anything more than a weakness. Gruits further agues that when God pardons our iniquities, he casts them into the depths of the sea, never to be remembered against us or our seed. Kylstra defines iniquity as the tendency to break God's heart with lawlessness, wickedness, unrighteousness, transgression or perversion.[133] If we are going duck hunting, we might as well shoot at everything. Kylstra

---

131 Patricia Beall Gruits, *Understanding God.* (Detroit, Michigan: Whitaker Books, 1972), 149.

132 Ibid, Gruits, 153.

133 Chester and Betsy Kylstra, *Restoring the Foundations.* (Henderson, NC: Proclaiming His Word Publications, 2001), 115.

also argues that everyone is under iniquity and that by confessing our iniquity, we can be cleansed from the iniquity, however iniquity remains on our seed until they individually repent of their iniquity.

Therefore, in summary of the sin of perversion, it is my conviction that wrong beliefs distort the truth, but what is so sinister about iniquity is that it becomes generational very easily. The historical reality of people following the beliefs of their forefathers for generations is based on the principle that children believe their parents teach them truth, and therefore rarely question those beliefs. The Lord visits to either bless or to punish, therefore when the Lord visits the iniquity to the 3rd and 4th generation, it is not to punish but rather he visits these generations with the Spirit of truth; that the generational line be cut off from the perversion. God's heart desire is never to curse but to eradicate the perversion in people's hearts.

When a person is **guilty** of perversion, whether it is perverting the truth of the gospel or perverting the laws instituted by the courts, there are consequences. Like most people, I know people who repented of a perversion when the truth was made known. I also know people who will never repent of their perversion and take them to the grave.

In summary of these four sins: ignorance, shortcoming, rebellion and perversion, I have once again chosen to use a model similar to Myers-Briggs.

The child is an easy example of ignorance, for we all come into this world with no knowledge and learn right from wrong. A good example today of ignorance is a lack of knowledge such as not knowing how to cook because you have not been taught. It is not wrong, just something you have not learned.

The shortcoming is best represented by a bad driver, a person who has a driver's license thus proof they are knowledgeable of the law but by means of inattention or being late, they desperately take the chance and speed.

The rebellious person is best represented by the biker who openly defies the law, such as riding without a helmet. This is the guy who "does it my way," someone who does not follow the rules of proper conduct.

Lastly, the person who perverts is like the person who belongs to a cult like the Mormons or Jehovah Witnesses. The problem with perversion is that it is passed from generation to generation as truth. Perversion is not limited to cults, though they provide an easy example. When Calvin introduced his concept of limited grace, he was declaring that Christ only died for those he had predestined to enter the kingdom. This is a perversion of the belief that Christ died for all people, that all people are created with a free will to accept or reject Christ.

I have chosen graphically to display the unknowing and untrained child in ignorance, as opposite of the well-aware, but stubborn, biker who rebels against the rules. The bad driver who attempts but fails to keep the law is opposite the person who perverts the law of grace, such as the cults. Like the Myers-Briggs model, it is a generalization only.

Graphically, the words for these four sins would appear like:

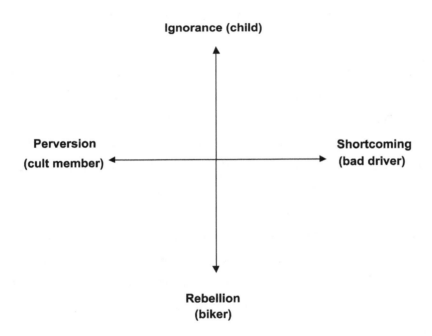

Chapter 11

THE COURT ADJUDICATED SINS

T he sins that had a corresponding sacrifice restored
the relationship between God and man, but there are
a number of sins which primarily mar the relationship people
have with other people. For these sins, a court system was
developed by Moses to settle the conflict between people,
and I have chosen to call the "Court Adjudicated Sins".
Human nature, being what it is, people soon discovered
ways to impede justice. Similarly, marriages often failed by
unfaithfulness, people learned to always carry a grudge,
while others would train their children their evil ways, thus
propagating sin from generation to generation, which is
called iniquity.

1.   The Sin of Injustice

This sin concerns a corruption of justice, someone using
the judicial system to take advantage of someone else. The
Hebrew word for injustice is the word "awal" (pronounced
"awe-wall"). It is found 21 times in the OT and is most often
interpreted as "iniquity, unjust, or unrighteous". The key

verse is found in Leviticus 19. Moses commanded Israel that no one was to corrupt the courts, that they are to do no injustice (awal) in judgment and that they will not be partial to the poor or the great; but in righteousness, judge their neighbor (Lev. 19:15).

It is only found 2 times before the Law in the Book of Job. Elihu said to Job that far be it from God that he should do wickedness, commit iniquity (injustice) or pervert judgment (justice) (Job 34:10,12). Job answered Elihu that he had imagined Job's sins, but if he had done iniquity (injustice) as Elihu had accused him of, Job was willing to do it no more (Job 34:32).

The word injustice is only found twice in Leviticus and twice in Deuteronomy. Moses further instructed that there was to be no injustice by manipulating the measurement system by false weights, volumes or scales, but they were to have just balances, just weights, just ephahs and just hins (Lev. 19:35). This is repeated for merchants who exchanged goods out of their own houses that they were not to have numerous weights or measures, for all that do such things are unrighteous (injustice) before the Lord (Deut. 25:13-16). Even the name of the Lord is defined by this word, for he is a rock, his work is perfect, all his ways are judgment (just); a God of truth and without iniquity (injustice), because just and right is he (Deut. 32:4). Though the KJV uses the term "iniquity" (awon), it does not exist in the verse. A better translation would be, "A God whose ways are justice, steadfast without injustice, holy and right is he."

The psalmist declares the anguish of David regarding his enemy; a man of the tribe of Benjamin called Cush, who accused David of injustice. David declared that if he was **guilty**, because there was iniquity (injustice) in his hands, he would be **guilty** of rewarding evil to someone who was at peace with him (Ps. 7:3,4). The psalmist asks how long will they judge unjustly (injustice) by accepting wicked persons, but defend the poor, fatherless and do justice to the afflicted and needy (Ps. 82:2-4). The fool has said in his heart, there is no God; they have become corrupt and have committed abominable iniquity (injustice) (Ps. 53:2). The fool's argument is that since God is not watching, he cannot punish their injustice. The unjust man is an abomination to the just; and he that is upright in the way is abomination to the wicked (Prv 29:27).

The only prophets to use this word are Jeremiah and Ezekiel. Jeremiah, in his first rebuke over Judah, spoke the word of the Lord, demanding the people give an answer to God for what iniquity (injustice) had their fathers found in him, that they had gone far from him and walked after vanity (Jer. 2:5). Again, the KJV uses the word iniquity (awon), which is not in this verse but rather "injustice", therefore the Lord is saying, "What injustice have your fathers seen in me that you would walk away from me toward vanities upon vanities?" The prophet Ezekiel defines the penalty of injustice by stating that when a righteous man turned from his righteousness and committed iniquity (injustice), the Lord would lay a stumbling block before him, and he will die. However, because you had not given him warning, he will die in his sin and his righteousness, which he has done will not be remembered, but his blood will I require at your hand (Ezek 3:20). The Lord's love for the righteous is such that when a righteous man commits an act of injustice, the Lord lays a stumbling block before him to prove him, for if he does not repent, he will die for his transgression. Ezekiel further defines the actions of the just person. If a just man does that which is lawful and right and has not oppressed any, but has restored to the debtor his pledge, he has not loaned with usury and has withdrawn his hand from iniquity (injustice), but has executed true judgment between men (Ezek 18:5,7-8).

As a covenant society that stressed justice between men and God, injustice struck at the core of the covenant. Robinson argued that "hesed" was derived from a fundamental concept of conformity to justice, but while often used to describe divine-human relations and translated as "grace". The word "grace" fails to portray loyalty, moral obligations and social bonds, which are the background of "hesed".[134] Gunkel argued that the "hesed" of Yahweh is not to be understood as grace, favor or kindness, but rather

---

134   H. Wheeler Robinson, *Inspiration and Revelation in the Old Testament.* (Oxford: Oxford Press, 1964), 57.

a covenantal relationship of reciprocal loyalty.[135] Therefore, injustice caused a rip in the fabric of society and a rip in the worship of God.

In the NT, the word for injustice is "adikos" (pronounced "haa-dee-koss"), it occurs 90 times in the LXX and 12 times in the NT, and is most commonly translated as "unjust" or "unrighteous". Referring to the key verse for injustice, the LXX reads that no one was to corrupt the courts, that they are to do no injustice (adikos) in judgment and that they will not be partial to the poor or the great; but in righteousness, judge their neighbor (Lev. 19:15).

Jesus, in the Beatitudes, declares their Father in heaven makes his sun to rise on the evil and the good, and sends rain on the just and the unjust (injustice) (Matt. 5:45). In the parable of the unjust steward, Jesus said he that is faithful in that which is least is faithful also in much, he that is unjust (injustice) in the least is unjust (injustice) also in much. If you have not been faithful (injustice) in the unrighteous mammon, who will commit to your trust the true riches (Lk 16:10,11)? The word "mammon" refers to wealth, property.[136] The Pharisee stood and prayed to himself, thanking God that he was not like other men: extortioners, unjust (injustice), adulterers or even like a publican (Lk 18:11).

---

135   Hermann Gunkel, *Genesis* (Gottingen: 1910), 253.

136   Frederick William Danker, *A Greek-English Lexicon.* (Chicago: University of Chicago Press, 2000), 614.

In Paul's defense before Felix, "that after the way which they called heresy he worshiped having hope toward God. That there will be a resurrection of the dead, both of the just and the unjust" (injustice) (Acts 24:15). Paul further argued that God was not unrighteous (injustice) for taking vengeance, for God will judge the world (Rom 3:5). Paul instructs Christians not to take one another to law before the unjust (injustice) but before the saints, reminding them the saints will judge the world (1 Cor 6:1).

The writer of Hebrews speaks of the things that accompany salvation; for God is not unrighteous (injustice) to forget your work and labor of love, which you have showed toward his name in that you have ministered to the saints (Heb 6:11).

Peter declared that Christ has once suffered for sins (shortcomings), the just for the unjust (injustice), that he might bring us to God, being put to death in the flesh but quickened by the Spirit (1 Pet. 3:18). Though Christ paid the price for injustice, there remains punishment for those who do not repent of injustice, the Lord knows how to deliver the godly out of temptations, and to reserve the unjust (injustice) unto the day of judgment to be punished (2 Pet. 2:9).

The idea here is that the injustice was not by a stranger but by someone trusted, which is like salt in a wound. The reason injustice is so much more generational than other evil is that because someone used the court system by means of perjury or theft to steal property or assets, thus greatly diminishing the state a man could pass onto the next generation, these future generations were hampered in developing wealth because the original wealth base was taken away. In addition, future generations of those who stole were under the curse of a thief and could not prosper.

In summary, those **guilty** of the sin of injustice can be recognized in three areas. First, it is the use of false weights and volume measurements to make financial advantage of someone else. Second, it is the ill treatment of the defense-less, such as the poor, the widow and the orphan, often by means of usury. Third, it is use of the courts to take advantage of someone else by means of false or insufficient testimony.

2.   The Sin of Treachery

This sin is described by the Hebrew word "bagod" (pro-nounced "baugh-goad"). This word is found 48 times in the OT and means to be without faith. This word is defined as "faithless, treachery, deception".[137] The key verse for this word is, "Surely as a wife treacherously (bagod) departs from her husband, so have you treacherously (bagod) with me, O House of Israel, says the Lord" (Jer. 3:20). This word is not found before the Law, it is found only once in Exodus,

---

137   F. Brown, S. Driver, C. Briggs, *The Brown-Driver-Briggs Hebrew and English Lexicon*, (Peabody, Mass.: Hendrickson, 2003), 93.

but it is not found in Leviticus, Numbers or Deuteronomy, therefore there is no scriptural reference of a sacrifice for treachery.

This word is first found in the instructions of Moses regarding slavery. If a female slave is betrothed to her master, and he changes his mind, he cannot sell her to a foreign people but she must be redeemed by her family, seeing that he has deceitfully (treacherously) dealt with her. If he takes another wife, her food, her clothing and her duty of marriage, he cannot diminish (Ex 21:8-10). Therefore the man, though he purchased a slave woman to marry, she had the rights of a married woman and his unwillingness to give her those rights constituted treachery.

Though Gideon had delivered Israel from the Midianites, the men of Shechem did not honor his family for the men of Shechem had dealt faithlessly (treacherously) with Abimelech (Judg. 9:23). King Saul gave a command that his men were not to eat before the battle ended, but his son Jonathan did not hear the command and ate some honey to strengthen him. However, many became faint and rushed to eat sheep, but in their hurry also ate the blood. When Saul was told this, he told the people they had transgressed (treachery) (1 Sam. 14:33). The people were so hungry that they could not wait to properly cook the food, thus transgressing the law, but Saul saw it as being unfaithful because they were not willing to remain in the battle.

Isaiah has a vision of the invading army of Sennacherib, a grievous vision declared to me, the treacherous dealer deals treachery and the spoiler spoils (Isa. 21:2). Every invading army had different tactics and a different system of rule, once they conquered a county. The Babylonians were known for treachery in keeping covenants. Isaiah brings two indictments against Israel; that from of old their ear has not been opened, and that they would deal very faithlessly (treacherously), because from birth they were called rebels (Isa. 48:8).

Jeremiah compares Israel and Judah as sisters, for Judah saw that for all the adulteries of faithless (treacherous) Israel, that the Lord had sent her away with a decree of divorce; yet her sister, Judah, did not fear, but she also went and played the harlot (Jer. 3:8). The Lord tells Jeremiah that Israel with apostasy has shown herself more faithless (treacherous) than Judah (Jer. 3:11). Jeremiah laments over living with his own people and desires that he might leave his people and go from them, for they are all adulterers (treacherous), an assembly of treacherous men (Jer. 9:2). Jeremiah complains to the Lord that the wicked are happy and prosperous, and even his own family who hate him deal treacherously against him. Why does the way of the wicked (treachery) prosper? Why are they happy who deal very treacherously, for even your brothers, the house of your father, even they have dealt treacherously with you (Jer. 12:1,6)?

Hosea explained the Lord departed because they had dealt faithlessly (treacherously) with the Lord and they have borne alien children (Hos 5:7). Habakkuk praises the Lord as holy, one who has established them for correction, one who has purer eyes than to behold evil and cannot look on iniquity. He then complains the Lord looks on them that deal treacherously and holds his tongue when the wicked devour the man that is more righteous than him (Hab. 1:13). Malachi tells the people we have one Father who created us, yet we deal treacherously every man against his brother by profaning the covenant of our fathers (Mal 2:10).

Regarding the NT, the Greek word that corresponds to "bagod" is the word "asunthetos" (pronounced "awe-sun-thee-toss"), and is only found once in the NT. The word is used by Paul, in his address to the Romans, when he speaks of men who changed the truth of God into a lie, and worshipped and served the creature more than the Creator (Rom 1:25). Paul declared they did not desire to retain God in their knowledge, so God gave them over to a reprobate mind (Rom 1:28). They were filled with all unrighteousness, fornication, wickedness and covetousness. They were without understanding, they were covenant-breakers (asunthetos), they had no natural affections and were unmerciful. Though they knew the judgment of God that those who commit such things were worthy of death, they not only did the same, but had pleasure in doing them (Rom 1:32).

In summary of the sin of treachery, this is a relational trespass, a breaking of covenant often by means of indifference. The person is **guilty** in their blindness to their indifference and cannot see their trespass. They occasionally go to the altar to get atonement, but their lives are not changed. Their minds are simply appeased of the guilt.

3.   The Sin of Offense

The word here is "asham" (pronounced "awe-sham). It is found 19 times in the OT and means "offense or wrongdoing".[138] The key verse is found in the narrative of a prophet by the name of Obed. When King Pekah of Israel went to war against King Ahaz of Judah, and after capturing many people of Judah were taking them into Israel, Obed the prophet stopped them and said:

> "You shall not bring the captives here, for whereas we have offended (asham) against the Lord already, you intend to add more to our sins (chata) and to our trespass (asham) for our trespass (asham) is great, and there is fierce wrath against Israel" (2 Chr 28:13).

---

138   F. Brown, S. Driver, C. Briggs, *The Brown-Driver-Briggs Hebrew and English Lexicon.* (Peabody, Mass.: Hendrickson, 2003), 79.

The taking of fellow Hebrews by Israel was such an offense to the Lord that if the prisoners were not immediately set free, they would suffer great wrath from God.

In a psalm by David, he cries that God knew his foolishness, and his sins (offenses) were not hid from him (Ps. 69:5).

After Jerusalem is destroyed, Ezra tears his clothes and plucks off his hair in despair, he laments that he is ashamed to lift his face to God, for their iniquities had increased over their head and their trespass (offenses) had grown up to the heavens (Ezr 9:6). Ezra recognizes that all that came upon them was because of their evil deeds and their trespass (offenses), acknowledging that God had punished them less than their iniquities deserved (Ezr 9:13). Ezra deals with the matter of interracial marriage and stood declaring they had transgressed by taking strange wives to increase the trespass (offense) of Israel (Ezr 10:10). The men were willing to repent, and they put away their wives; and being **guilty** (offense), they offered a ram of the flock for their trespass (offense) (Ezr 10:19). Here, the same word was translated into English as both guilt and trespass.

Satan provoked David to number Israel and David instructed Joab to number Israel, from Beersheba to Dan. Joab asked David why he required to number the population because Joab knew it would be a cause of trespass (offense) to Israel (1 Chr 21:1-3). After the death of King Jehoiada, Judah returned to apostasy, leaving the house of the Lord and serving groves and idols, so wrath came upon Judah and Jerusalem for their trespass (offense)(2 Chr 24:18). King Amon reigned in Jerusalem, but did that which was evil like Manasseh his father, sacrificing unto all the carved images and humbled not himself but trespassed (offended) more and more (2 Chr 33:21-23).

Offense as described by these verses are primarily a violation of rights between people; but because the people were covenant people, the offense also were a violation in heaven.

The Hebrew word "asham" is expressed by the Greek word "paraptoma" (pronounced "paa-rap-toe-mah"). It occurs 19 times in the NT and means "a violation of moral standards, offense, wrongdoing".[139] The key verse for "paraptoma" is, "For if you forgive men their trespasses (paraptoma), your heavenly Father will also forgive you" (Matt. 6:14, Mk 11:25). Too often, Christians ask their Heavenly Father to forgive offenses towards others, without asking the person they offended first.

Paul taught the Romans that death reigned from Adam to Moses, even over those who had not sinned like Adam's transgression, for if through the offence of one, many died (Rom 5:14). Paul adds Christ was delivered for our offences, and was raised again for our justification (Rom

---

139   F. Brown, S. Driver, C. Briggs, *The Brown-Driver-Briggs Hebrew and English Lexicon*, (Peabody, Mass.: Hendrickson, 2003), 770.

4:25). Regarding the Jews, Paul tells them that they stumbled not that they should fall, but rather through their fall (offence) salvation is come unto the Gentiles to provoke them to jealousy (Rom 11:11). Now if their fall (offence) are riches for the world, and their failure are riches for the Gentiles, how much more will be their fullness (Rom 11:12)? To the Corinthians, Paul declares that God was in Christ reconciling the world to himself, not imputing their trespasses (offences) to them; and has committed unto us the word of reconciliation (2 Cor 5:19). Regarding how we are to treat each other, if a man is overtaken in a fault (offence), you that are spiritual are to restore him in the spirit of meekness, considering yourself because you also can be tempted (Gal 6:1). Paul speaks of redemption, for in Christ we have redemption through his blood, the forgiveness of sins (offences) according to the riches of his grace (Eph 1:7) for he has quickened you who were dead in trespasses (offences) and sins (shortcomings) (Eph 2:1). Paul repeats this saying that even when we were dead in sins (offences), he quickened us together with Christ, by grace you are saved (Eph 2:5). And you, being dead in your sins (offences) and the uncircumcision of your flesh, he quickened you together with him, having forgiven you all trespasses (offences) (Col 2:13). Paul, therefore, sees not only the forgiveness of their shortcomings by missing the law, but also their offenses by ill-treating of one another.

In summary of the sin of offense, this sin creates a sinister current of contamination. The marriage of foreign wives offended the men who married according to the law. Civil war between the tribes of Israel greatly offended other tribes who were not a part of the conflict. The numbering of the people by the king offended those who looked to Yahweh Saboath as their protector. The salvation of those who did not deserve salvation became an offense to those who had separated their lives unto salvation.

Summary of the Court Adjudicated Sins

Considering the sins of injustice, treachery and offense, there are subtle differences between these three sins. The sin of injustice often is not recognized by those it oppresses; because a person purchasing food from a merchant who uses false weights or volumes may not be aware they are being taken advantage of. The ill treatment of the poor, the widow or the orphan was often so common that these people just expected to be treated that way. A bad judgment of a court by means of false testimony was often perceived as bad luck. The sin of treachery by means of breaking covenant often led to indifference, the person gradually becomes hardened though they may appease their guilt by sacrifice or good works. However, the sin of offense is much more devious in that it spreads like wildfire, offending everyone in the community. The prophet Malachi declared that God hates divorce (Mal 2:16), yet Moses made provision for divorce. I am of the opinion that God hates divorce because it does not contaminate two people, but parents, siblings, children, friends and even distant relatives all become contaminated as they take sides in the divorce conflict. God then has a contaminated community and not just two people to heal. Recent public surveys of the attitudes of the citizens of San Francisco reveal that though there remains a low percentage of people who are homosexual, there is a high acceptance of homosexual rights, and therefore people outside the homosexual community become offensive about homosexual rights that they do not appropriate in their own lives.

As I have examined the three general concepts of sin, the unforgivable sins, the forgivable sins and the judicial sins, there appears to be an interrelationship between them all.

The Mustard Seed

Most people are familiar of the teaching of Jesus that, "faith is like a mustard seed". I would suggest that sin is identical to faith and, therefore, sin is also like a mustard seed.

> "The kingdom of heaven is like a grain of mustard seed, which a man took, and sowed in his field. Which indeed is the least of all seeds, but when it is grown, it is the greatest among the herbs, and becomes a tree, so that the birds of the air come and lodge in the branches thereof" (Matt. 13:31-32).

"If you have faith as a grain of mustard seed, you shall say unto this mountain, Remove hence to yonder place; and it shall remove; and nothing shall be impossible unto you" (Matt. 17:20)

There has been some controversy over this parable, since there are plants with slightly smaller seeds and the tree only grows to a height of about 12 feet. However, in the minds of the people of Palestine, it was the smallest commercial seed and small birds often perched on its limbs. Nevertheless, I believe it is a good analogy of both faith and sin. Like faith, sin begins with the smallest of thought, which later is acted upon, becoming an action. Like faith, it must be cultivated because left to its own will wither and die. Like faith, sin can grow to a great size. No one is born a murderer, but rather attitudes, actions and opportunities create an atmosphere in order to bring about the serious action of murder. In addition, there seems to be a line that one must cross in order to step into a more serious crime. Police know that petty thieves and street hustlers are often non-violent, and only a serious confrontation would cause that person to kill someone, but once one murder is committed, it is much easier to commit murder again. It is as if there has been a promotion in the spirit realm to a greater realm of sin. Satanists pay considerable sums of money to advance into higher realms of demonic authority. Therefore, I have created a graph to demonstrate how these three sin concepts interact, that just as someone can advance into greater sin by their actions, so by repentance they can also retreat.

The Sin Pyramid

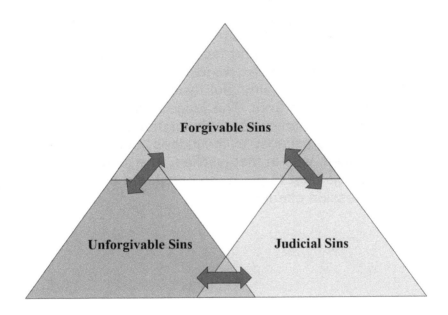

This pyramid shows the relationship between the three classes of Hebraic sins. Though sin in any area can result in eternal separation from God, the most severe sin group is the unforgivable sins. No sin acts alone, therefore there is often strong correlations and fluidity between these groups of sin. An example:

A forgivable sin such as stealing a piece of food brings the thief before the judges. But the person who was stolen from wrongfully testifies before the judges that the thief stole much more than he did. The judges rule the thief to pay the man he stole from double. However, bitterness sets as the thief struggles to pay the fine. In time the thief, in anger, kills the man he stole from. He has now committed an unforgivable sin and faces the death penalty. At this point, another witness comes forth and testifies as to the wrongful testimony of the man who was stolen from. The judges rule that since his false testimony was worthy of death, his death, though not prescribed by the judges but carried out by the thief, was in fact justified. The judges now instruct the thief to go to the priest and offer up a transgression offering.

Chapter 12
THE LEVITICAL OFFERINGS AND THE ATONEMENT

S ince the destruction of the Temple in 70 AD, the Jews have not been able to offer sacrifices. For Christians, Christ is our great sacrifice and we enter his presence based upon the shed blood of Christ. We appropriate our healing through his shed blood. But much of the imagery and function of the old priesthood continues because it was a pattern for the new covenant. Like the Jews, all Christians come before the Lord equal, position or wealth have no significance for his forgiveness. Likewise, when we offend others, our cry for forgiveness is not answered until we first mend the offence and restore the relationship. And lastly, the nature of our sin determines our payment. Sin always has a cost, even when it is forgiven.

A.   The Levitical Offerings for Sin
Haldeman argues that there are five offerings in the book of Leviticus, the burnt offering, the cereal offering, the

peace offering, the sin offering and the trespass offering.[140] The nature of the offerings was to cleanse for sin and was available to all, irrespective of wealth or position in society, and the type of offering reflected the seriousness of sin with no reflection of ability to pay, with the exception of the poor. It must be remembered that in order to offer an offering, a person must be allowed to enter the temple, which was forbidden by two groups of people: people of other nations that were not Jews and people who had committed unforgivable sins, such as murder or witchcraft.

1)   The Burnt Offering

This offering was a mature male ox or bull with horn, its blood was sprinkled about the altar, it was skinned, cut into pieces, the fat was separated and was fully consumed with fire. Bonar argued that the wealthy were required to offer bulls, the ordinary folk offered sheep and the poor offered pigeons as burnt offerings.[141] However, I am under the conviction that the type of animal selected was in accordance with the nature of the sin, not in accordance of what they could afford. Though Moses made a provision for the poor so that no person would be denied the right to bring a sacrifice,

---

140   I.M. Haldeman, *The Tabernacle Priesthood and Offerings*, (New Jersey: Fleming Revell Company, 1925), 324.

141   Andrew Bonar, *A Commentary on the Book of Leviticus.* (Grand Rapids: Baker Books, 1978), 21.

there is little scriptural evidence the type of sacrifice was in accordance to wealth.

2)   The Cereal Offering

Also called the Meat Offering, this was a bloodless offering baked as an unleavened cake comprising of fine flour. Oil was poured on the flour, frankincense was put on the oil and it was seasoned with salt. This was a first fruits offering that was baked, not burnt, and was shared by the person who brought the offering and the priests. Everyone brought the same offering, regardless of wealth or position in society, and it was consumed along with the peace offering in the temple area.

3)   The Peace Offering

This is a thanksgiving offering that was a male or female lamb or goat that was roasted on the altar, with both the priests and the person who brought the offering shared; each got half to eat. The person bringing their lamb waited for it to be cooked and, along with the cereal offering, ate it at the temple site before returning home.

4)   The Sin Offering

Bonar argues that this offering is for sins of ignorance. The average person offered a young bull, the ruler offered a goat and the priests offered a ram to cover sins of ignorance; whereas the poor offered two pigeons. These sacrifices indicate that specific offices such as the rulers and the priests had unique offerings, not due to wealth but due to the nature of their office to be distinguished apart from ordinary folk. This offering was a yearly event. The High Priest entered the Holies of Holies once a year for the sins of ignorance for the people.

5)   The Trespass Offering

Leviticus 14 describes the actions of the priests for a trespass offering. The priest would take water, oil and blood, and touch the right ear, right thumb and right toe. The blood was to forgive, the water to cleanse and the oil to anoint. The right ear so the man could hear God, the right thumb so the man would do the works of God and the right toes so the man would walk in the ways of God. The purpose of the sacrifice was not to just get rid of the sin, but to re-establish the person's covenant with God. Bonar states that this offering is for broken fellowship, the **guilty** must make restoration for the sin committed and adds a fifth part to the principal of that which he took away, or in which he caused loss or wrong to another.[142] The penalty was not based on wealth, but rather on the value of the goods stolen, broken or lost. Bonar argues that for those suffering from a sickness, such as leprosy, once they have been pronounced clean by the priest, they brought a male lamb for a trespass (asham)

---

142   Andrew Bonar, *A Commentary on the Book of Leviticus.* (Grand Rapids: Baker Books, 1978), 103

offering, a male lamb for a sin (kata) offering and a cereal offering (Lev. 14:10).[143] Though a provision is made for the poor, all others with leprosy made the same offering, therefore there was no relation between sacrifice and wealth. Rather, Yahweh had promised that the Israelites would not have the diseases of Egypt, so this requirement of providing sacrifices after a person is healed from a disease strongly implies a link between disease and sin.

It must be remembered that in ancient Israel that stonings were rare. That is why when King Saul met with the witch of Endor she knew the death penalty for her actions, yet lived unharmed. Though the penalties for the unpardonable sins are harsh, they did not stone you at a mere accusation, but reserved judgment until there was ample proof, your sin had become a lifestyle. I am convinced that the eleven Hebrew words for sins did not constitute a single action, but a lifestyle that one day an action that had occurred often was the tipping point for judgment. This raises the question, "If some who have done heinous sin and have been forgiven, what is the measuring stick?" What constitutes forgiveness for an unforgivable sin? I have the conviction the answer lies in an understanding of the atonement.

B. The Atonement

---

143   Ibid, Bonar, 264.

There are a number of theories regarding the atonement. Erickson states that the atonement is the transition point from the objective doctrines of God, such as the doctrine of sin to the subjective doctrine, which balances theology so that it can be relevant to the believer.[144] I have presented an objective view of eleven sin concepts and how each concept was represented by a word that I believe is an accurate understanding of that word, however, before I can make an application for the church today, an examination of the atonement is necessary to move from the objective doctrine of sin to a subjective relevant view.

Erickson gives an excellent overview of the interconnectedness of the various facets of salvation. Salvation begins with our receiving a righteous standing before God (justification), the instilling of spiritual life, direction and vitality into our lives (regeneration), and matures by the development of godliness (sanctification).[145] But salvation begins with the atonement, for the atonement makes salvation possible. However, our beliefs about God, and sin, impact our understanding of God.

Faustus Socinus argued that the new covenant of Christ brings absolute forgiveness of all sin, because God does not demand any form of satisfaction of justice from

---

144   Millard Erickson, *Christian Theology*, (Grand Rapids: Baker Books, 1985), 798.

145   Millard Erickson, *Christian Theology*, (Grand Rapids: Baker Books, 1985), 800.

those who sin against him. He postulated that Christ was a perfect example of the type of dedication God desires of us. The problem with his theory is that he places such an emphasis on God's love that there is no place for outer darkness, no gnashing of teeth and no place of torment, of which Christ spoke of.

Peter Abelard, in his Moral Influence Theory of Atonement, argued that sin merely separates people from God; that God does not have to punish them, just push them away. Abelard says that the mission of Jesus was merely to heal souls and to remove our fear of God, because God responds to us with compassion and not condemnation.[146] However, Abelard fails to address the justice of God. At the opposite end of the scale, Hugo Grotius claimed that God as ruler has the right to punish sin. God cannot cancel debt like a creditor, or fail to punish like a master, but is bound to uphold every violation of the law. If all sin is freely forgiven, just for the asking, the authority and effectiveness of law is undermined. Sin is not punished as a means of retribution because it deserves to be punished, but the demands of moral government require a deterrence of further commission of sin.[147] Though I agree with Grotius that God, in every

---

146   Millard Erickson, Christian Theology, (Grand Rapids: Baker Books, 1985), 804.

147   Ibid, Erickson, 807.

case, requires a penalty equivalent to the offense, Groitus failed to imply what sins the death of Christ paid for.

Gregory of Nyssa taught that since the slavery, in which we find ourselves, is our own doing, our own free choice, it would have been unjust to deprive Satan of his captives by some arbitrary method. That would have been to steal from Satan what was rightfully his.[148] I agree that we have the potential to sell ourselves into the slavery of sin, but there is a vast difference between assumed ownership and legal ownership.

Lester Sumrall taught that there are seven steps, which Satan uses to take over a soul. They are regression, repression, suppression, depression, oppression, obsession and possession. These steps go from simple outward harassment of evil spirits to total control. The individual, by their free choice, would had to deliberately allowed themselves to progress from one step to another step. The last three steps involve such demonic control that the person is unable to free themselves and require others to help liberate them by means of deliverance. I believe there is little scriptural support to suggest that when we are born-again that we are immediately unshackled.

Kylstra teaches that born-again believers still bear the sins of their fathers with resulting curses, ungodly beliefs,

---

148   Ibid, Erickson, 811.

spirit and soul hurts, and demonic oppression.[149] This deliverance ministry has proven that Christians, though born-again, can have demons; and so Satan maintains an assumed ownership, though his legal ownership has been destroyed.

Christ saw his death as constituting a ransom (Matt. 20:28), he saw himself as our substitute (Jn 15:32), he saw himself in the role of sacrifice (Jn 17:19) and he saw himself as the work of the Father (Jn 6:38). George Ladd says that the idea that the cross expresses the love of Christ for us while he wrestles atonement from a stern and unwilling Father, whose justice is demanding and inflexible, is a perversion of New Testament Theology.[150] Traditionally it has been regarded that Christ's death was propitiatory, that is, Christ died to appease God's wrath against sin. However Dodd contends that it is not propitiatory, but rather expiation:

> "Whom God has set forth to be a propitiation (ilasterion) through faith in his blood, to declare his righteousness for the remission of sins (amartematon) that are past, through the forbearance of God" (Rom 3:25).

---

149   Chester and Betsy Kylstra, *Restoring the Foundations*. (Henderson, NC: Proclaiming His Word Publications, 2001), 7.

150   George Ladd, *A Theology of the New Testament*, (Grand Rapids: Eerdmans, 1974), 424.

The word "ilasterion" (pronounced "high-lass-terr-eye-on") means, "appeasement of sin, expiation".[151] The OT references use this word as "an instrument for appeasing by means of sacrifice." Dodd says that God was not appeased by the death of Christ, but rather what Christ accomplished in dying was to cleanse sinners of their sin, to cover their sins. The word "ilasterion" is only found one other time in the NT. "And over it the cherubims of glory shadowing the mercy seat (ilasterion) of which we cannot now speak particularly" (Heb 9:5). Though the KJV translates this word as "mercy seat", in context, this is when the High Priest entered the Holy of Holies once a year with blood for the errors (agnonmaton) of the people. As shown, this word means "sins of ignorance". Every man in the OT was required to offer a sacrifice for the sins he was aware of, but for sins the people were unaware of the High Priest covered once a year. The author of Hebrews not only states that the New High Priest, Jesus, covered the sins of ignorance, but for the redemption of the transgressions (parabaseon) also (Heb 9:15). I have shown this word to mean "offense". It is Hebrews 9:22 that most people skip over, "And almost (schedon) all things are by the law purged with blood." The

---

151   Frederick William Danker, *A Greek-English Lexicon of the New Testament and other Early Christian Literature*, 3d ed, (Chicago: University of Chicago, 2000), 474.

word "schedon" means, "nearly, almost, but not all".[152] Note that it does not say all things but "almost" all things, for there were sins that had no atonement for in the OT, which is reflected by the author of Hebrews:

> "So Christ was once offered to bear the sins (amartia) of many, and unto them that look for him shall appear the second time, without sin (amartia) unto salvation" (Heb 9:28).

Our beliefs about God and sin impact our understanding of God. If a person believes the word "sin" means every wrong deed, then they would believe that the atonement covers every wrong deed, however great. For those that believe "sin" means those deeds which by example of the Israelites had covered by sacrifice, then they would believe Christ's sacrifice does not cover all sins.

---

152   Frederick William Danker, *A Greek-English Lexicon of the New Testament and other Early Christian Literature*, 3d ed, (Chicago: University of Chicago, 2000), 981.

Chapter 13

THEOLOGY FOR TODAY

T here have been many attempts over the past 2,000 years to define the concept of sin, and today believers are no different than those who have gone on ahead. Henry Thiessen argued there were 4 sets of sins:

1) Sin of nature – the guilt that comes from inborn sin.

2) Sins of ignorance or sins of knowledge – the greater the knowledge of sin, the greater the guilt.

3) Sins of weakness and sins of presumption – the amount of the strength of the will indicates the degree of guilt.

4) Sins of incomplete and sins of hardheartedness – the degree to which the soul has hardened itself and become unreceptive to multiplied offers of grace determines the degree of guilt.[153]

Yet this still does not define sin adequately, it only defines sin as the cause of guilt, however guilt can be misleading. If two people are overeating at a buffet, one may feel **guilty**

---

153   Henry Thiessen, *Lectures in Systematic Theology.* (Grand Rapids: Eerdmans, 1979), 193.

because they ate so much as to become sick, but the other person may feel **guilty** because they broke a diet. Thus guilt is often a relational feeling that may have little to do with actual sin. Erickson defines sin as the evil of war, crime, cruelty, class struggles, discrimination, slavery and injustice.[154] That may well define sin today, but believers just 200 years ago saw no wrong in slavery. Today, many consider smoking as a sin because so many have died of lung cancer, but sin is not defined as something that causes illness. Puritans saw tobacco as a form of wealth and a blessing from God. Therefore, sin has traditionally been defined by preachers with their personal worldview as they search scripture to support their beliefs, resulting in a panorama of ideas of what actually constitutes sin. My conviction is that the Israelites understood sin conceptually much different than we do today. Moses declared to the Israelites, "Today I set before you life and death, choose life!" Christ declared that he was the light of men. Paul declared that the Hebrews were ensamples. Therefore, we seriously consider all scripture that we might learn and walk in the light.

---

154   Millard Erickson, *Christian Theology*. (Grand Rapids: Baker Books, 1985), 412.

1.   A View of the Unforgivable Sin

Ask most Christians, "What is the unforgivable sin?" and they will say "Blasphemy of the Holy Ghost." Known as the "Unpardonable Sin", it is recorded in the Gospel of Matthew:

> "Wherefore I say unto you, all manner of sin and blasphemy shall be forgiven unto men; but the blasphemy against the Holy Ghost shall not be forgiven unto men. And whosoever speaks a word against the Son of man, shall be forgiven him; but whosoever speaks against the Holy Ghost; it shall not be forgiven him, neither in this world, neither in the world to come" (Matt. 12:31-32).

The two key words of Jesus in this verse are "sin" and "blasphemy". The word for sin is the word "amartia" and the word for blasphemy is "blasphemia", which means "speech that denigrates, defames, slanders, or disrespects".[155] Jesus had just healed a man possessed with the devil, but when the Pharisees heard of it, they accused Jesus of casting out the devil by Beelzebub. If anyone knew what the death penalty sins were, it was the Pharisees. If indeed Jesus declared that it was the only sin that was unpardonable, the Pharisees would had the right to stone him. Yet Jesus knew the Word of God, for he literally embodied it. As Christians, we consider the gospels to be NT, but in reality the OT ends

---

155   Frederick William Danker, *A Greek-English Lexicon*. (Chicago: University of Chicago Press, 2000), 178

with the cross and the NT does not start until the day of the resurrection of Christ. Without the death and resurrection of Christ, there would be no Christianity. Therefore since it remains OT, the law of Moses was in full force. For Jesus to say that only blasphemy against the Holy Ghost was pardonable when murder, witchcraft and other sins were death penalty sins, he was either telling a lie or our understanding of this verse is wrong. In context, Jesus was declaring that to the pile of death penalty sins that could not be forgiven, he was adding one more; blasphemy against the Holy Ghost.

Most TV evangelists will tell you that Jesus forgives every sin. Though that may sound wonderful, it is not scriptural. I believe that every sin stands until it receives forgiveness. Jesus is not our "Santa Claus", handing out gifts of repentance, nor did Jesus forgive your every sin on the cross. If Jesus forgave your every sin on the cross, you would have no reason to ever say "sorry" or ask for repentance. It is only when, with a sorrowful heart, we covenant with our Lord to change our behavior that we can receive forgiveness.

One of the attributes of Yahweh is that he is immutable, he does not change. Even the death and resurrection of his son, Jesus Christ, did not change his character. Christians declare that Christ is equal with the Father (Apostles Creed), yet we have this belief that there is no sin that Jesus will not forgive. As I have clearly shown, there are unforgivable sins.

Therefore our understanding of the Trinity must come into alignment with our understanding of sin.

It was John Calvin who developed the "tulip" principle, believing that since God knew the beginning from the end, God knew who was born for salvation and who was born for damnation.[156] The acronym "t.u.l.i.p." stood for total depravity, unconditional predestination, limited atonement, irresistible grace and perseverance.[157] Thus Calvin believed man was so totally depraved, he was unable to get saved except by divine intervention. Calvin believed some people were born to go to hell. Calvin believed if you were predestined to go to heaven, you could not resist in getting saved. For Calvin, salvation was limited and that Christ only died for those who would be saved. Calvin's theology was dominate in many churches for more than 300 years, but thankfully is rejected by most churches today. Like Calvin, it would be very easy for me to postulate a new theory on what sins Jesus died for. It is with reservation that I postulate the following theory:

- God the Father, creator of all has not changed, even the birth of the Church has not changed his moral stand regarding sin. God the Father still sees murder, homosexuality, child sacrifice and witchcraft as death penalty sins.

---

156   Alister McGrath, *The Christian Theology Reader*. (Oxford: Blackwell Publishers, 2110), 426.

157   Millard Erickson, *Christian Theology*. (Grand Rapids: Baker Books, 2000), 929.

- Sins such as murder still place a curse on the land.
- Sins still pass down the generations as curses.
- Christ is now our heavenly High Priest (Heb 5:10).
- Christ entered the holy place with his own blood and has obtained eternal redemption for us (Heb 9:12).
- Christ is mediator of a better covenant (Heb 8:6), not a replacement covenant.
- Christ is a minister in the heavenly sanctuary and the heavenly tabernacle, not built by men (Heb 8:3)
- Just as the blood of bulls and goats sprinkled the unclean to the purifying of the flesh, how much more the blood of Christ purges our conscience (Heb 9:14)?
- Just as the Israelite High Priest offered no sacrifice for sins unto death, but only sacrifices for those sins the could be redeemed, Christ likewise redeems only those sins of ignorance, shortcoming, rebellion, perversion, injustice, treachery and offense.
- There is no redemption of sins such as murder, homosexuality and witchcraft.

The real fear of this type of theology is that radical, anti-homosexual groups may use it as fuel for hatred. Pastor Fred Phelps of the Westboro Baptist Church in Topeka, Kansas is known for his radical use of flags that say, "God hates fags." Recent court challenges by the homosexual community force churches to be silent on the subject. A gag order is not the answer. Therefore, a middle ground must be reached, a position where the extremes of giving no eternal hope to those who have committed unforgivable sins and the position that Christ forgives every sin known to mankind.

Jesus declared that those that believed on his name would be saved (Jn 3:16-18, Rom 5:6-10). Salvation is entrance into the kingdom of God and the promise of eternal life. However, the person who has committed an unforgivable sin, salvation may not be lost but the penalty remains. In the story about how Jesus healed the Centurion's son, Jesus declared that many would come from the East and the West into the kingdom, but the children of the kingdom would be cast into outer darkness (Matt. 8:12). They remained in the kingdom, but were in darkness.

Rick Joyner writes about a heavenly experience where the outer regions of heaven are like darkness in comparison to the areas close to the throne. According to Joyner, there are levels of heaven with the levels decreasing in brightness and glory as they are further from the throne of God. Therefore, the lowest level remains in heaven, but has much less light.

Jesus also declared in the Parable of the Tares that the field is the world, the good seed is of the son but the tares are of the evil one (Matt. 13:36). The KJV implies the tares belong to Satan, but the description "evil one", is "ponerou", which means "socially worthless, degenerate";[158] not "Satana", which is "Satan" (Matt. 16:23). This implies those that sowed the tares are children of evil men, that is, a generational evil. The angels will gather those in the kingdom who offend (skandala) and do iniquity (anomia), that they would be cast into fire (kaminon) (Matt. 13:37-42). Note; they are cast into "kaminon", a word used to describe a oven or potter's kiln.[159] They are not cast into hellfire (gehenna), as in Matt. 18:9, but a furnace. In the Parable of Fishnet, Jesus declared that his angels would separate the wicked (ponerous) from the just and cast the wicked (poneros) into the furnace of fire (kaminon) (Matt. 13:49-50). In the Parable of the Marriage Feast, the King demands to know why a guest is not dressed in a wedding garment (Matt. 22:12). The man is not cast into hell, but cast into outer darkness. In the Parable of the Fig Tree, the evil servant is sent to a place of weeping and gnashing of teeth (Matt. 24:48-51). In the parable of the Unprofitable Servant, the unprofitable (achreion) servant is sent into outer darkness (skotia) with weeping and gnashing of teeth (Matt. 25:30). The word "achreion" means "worthless", but has a component of a continuous action up to a point in time, that is, not originally

158   Frederick William Danker, *A Greek-English Lexicon*. (Chicago: University of Chicago Press, 2000), 851.

159   Ibid, Danker, 506.

worthless but becoming worthless.[160] The word "skotia" means, "devoid of light, darkness, absence of sunlight".[161] Once again, the penalty is that the person went into outer darkness, not hell.

Jesus declared that anyone who believed on his name would be saved. In the Gospel of Mark, Jesus said, "He that believes and is baptized will be saved; but he that believes not will be damned" (Mk 16:16). John opens his gospel by declaring, "He came unto his own, and his own received him not, but as many as received him, to them gave he power to become the sons of God, even to them that believe on his name (Jn 1:12). John closes his gospel with the same promise, "But these are written, that ye might believe that Jesus is the Christ, the Son of God; and that believing ye might have life through his name" (Jn 20:31). Lastly, John closes his epistle with, "These things have I written unto you that believe on the name of the Son of God; that ye may know that ye have eternal life, and that ye may believe on the name of the Son of God" (1 Jn 5:3). I absolutely agree that believing on the name of Christ ushers a person into the Kingdom of God. However, there are both prerequisites to entering the Kingdom of God and membership has covenant responsibility that does not negate the possibility of penalty. Though no ethnic people group is excluded, all people groups

---

160   Ibid, Danker, 160.

161   Ibid, Danker, 931.

are offered salvation, salvation is not available to all. If a person wants to be an engineer or medical doctor, they must, by law, attend university and pass exams that qualify then to practice engineering or medicine. There is no exclusion based on race and once they begin their career, but gross negligence will cause the stripping of their designation and prevent them from continuing to work in that field.

The concept that Christ did not die for unforgivable sins raises the question about Moses, David and Paul. Moses was buried by Yahweh in a valley in Moab (Deut. 34:6), but the devil argued over the body of Moses (Jude 9). This strongly suggests that Satan had legal claim over his body because Moses had killed the Egyptian, and that God had to privately bury Moses. Nathan accused David of killing Uriah (2 Sam. 12:9), but the sin came with a penalty, his child by Bathsheba would die so that the heathen would not blaspheme the name of the Lord. The Lord required the penalty of the shedding of life, life for life and death for death, to be paid. The Lord gave both men a measure of grace, even though they had murdered. Regarding the Apostle Paul, his own testimony was that he persecuted the Christians; howbeit it was in ignorance (1 Tim. 1:13). To assume God would give the same grace to murderers today must be considered in the light that both men sought God's mercy with everything in their being. Police statistics show that overwhelmingly, most people who murder only kill one person and that is due to deep wounding; wounding often caused by continuous abuse. God sees the heart and is willing to pardon, but his pardon can never be considered automatic. Serial killers are rare, and those who kill for the thrill, or kill in accordance to religious duty, fall into a different category. I have the conviction that they have little hope of pardon.

Paul declared that in the fullness of time, Christ came to redeem them that were under the law that we might receive the adoption of sons (Gal 4:5) and, as sons, we are heirs of God led by the Spirit who do not participate in:

1)	Adultery		
2)	Fornication	"porneia"	sexual immorality
3)	Uncleanness	"akatharsia"	vileness
4)	Lasciviousness	"aselgeia"	indecent, lack of self-constraint
5)	Idolatry	"eidololatria"	worship of idols
6)	Witchcraft	"pharmuakeia"	sorcery
7)	Hatred	"echthrai"	enmity, hostility
8)	Variance	"eris"	strife, incite violence
9)	Emulations	"zelos"	jealousy, envy
10)	Wrath	"thumoi"	rage, indignation
11)	Strife	"eritheiai"	pursuit of office by unfair means, ambitious
12)	Seditions	"dichostasiai"	dissention, dividing parties
13)	Heresies	"aireseis"	faction, sect
14)	Envyings	"phthovoi"	corrupt, destroy
15)	Murders		
16)	Drunkenness	"methai"	unrestrained revelry, drunk
17)	Revellings	"komoi"	excessive feasting

The KJV adds "adultery" and "murder", but the Greek words "moicheuseis" (adultery)[162] and "phoneuseis" (murder)[163] are not in the original text (Gal 5:19-21). It may be futile to try to understand why the Puritans added adultery and divorce to the list. The only two acts in this list by Paul that would be unforgivable sins are idol worship and witchcraft, which is reasonable considering the idolatry and witchcraft of Rome. Therefore, this is not a list to expel persons from the faith, but a list of things that Christians should not get involved with because they can cause bondage (Gal 4:9).

Nevertheless, if this was the standard for churches today, most churches would close to non-attendance. What is interesting about this list is that Paul declares those that do them cannot inherit the kingdom of God. He then contrasts this list with the fruits of the Spirit, followed by advice on how to restore a believer who have been overtaken by a fault. Paul, therefore, is not stating that those who commit these faults cannot receive eternal salvation (Gal 5:21). Eternal salvation is based on faith, inheriting the kingdom of God is based on obedience to reject the faults of the world. I believe upon salvation that a believer enters the kingdom of God, the rule of God upon the earth. However, if the believer falls into sins and commits one of

---

162   Frederick William Danker, *A Greek-English Lexicon*. (Chicago: University of Chicago, 2000), 656.

163   Ibid, Danker, 1063.

the 15 sins above, it renders him ineffective in the kingdom of God. Hopefully, another believer restores him but if not, upon death, the believer still passes unto eternal life. It is at the Judgment Seat of Christ he must bear the judgment of those sins he has failed to repent of.

John Turner states that the polemic of 1 John views sin very seriously, that while believers do occasionally sin, they do not persist in ethical disobedience, social bigotry or christological heresy. In this qualified sense, they do not sin, in other words, their sin is not deadly. But those who walk in darkness while claiming to be in the light, who hate believers and who deny that Jesus is the Messiah, are committing deadly sins.[164] The Greek word for sin in 1 John is consistently "amartia", because it is a family letter from the Father to his little children who are in the world. The sin of a believer is treated as a child's offence and is dealt with as a family matter.

Dr. George Hill, founder of Victory Churches International, believes that few Christians sin so seriously as to lose their salvation, because the Holy Spirit leads to repentance. I agree with Hill that no Christian, though they should fall often, with a heart toward God should never fear loss of salvation.

---

164   David, L. Turner, *Baker Theological Dictionary of the Bible*, Walter A. Elwell, ed., (Grand Rapids: Baker Books, 1996), 740.

I do not follow Calvinist doctrine, however this study does point to limited atonement. The significant difference is that I do not believe that Christ only died for the godly, but all men. Rather all men have access to the atonement of Christ, but that atonement does not cover all sin, for if atonement covered all sin there would be no need of judgment.

Alcorn argues that one of the hardest questions we face is how to reconcile two paradoxical scriptural principles; forgiveness for sin and having to live with the consequences of sin. We must face the fact that the Bible clearly teaches both, and we must believe both, even if we do not understand how they can both be true.[165] Christ's blood cleanses us from sin's guilt, but it does not remove all of sin's consequences. Being forgiven does not change our accountability for what we have done. Alcom adds that not only does sin have consequences, but each time we sin, we reinforce a pattern that becomes harder and harder to break.[166]

Claybrook argued that the punishment for violation of the first covenant was physical death (Num. 15:30), but the punishment for rejecting the new covenant is spiritual death.[167] Few understand that this does not mean after death alone, but violation of God's principles cripple a

165   Randy Alcorn, *Christians in The Wake of the Sexual Revolution*, (Portland, Oregon: Multnomah Press, 1985). 240.

166   Ibid, Alcorn, 243.

167   Frederick Claybrook, *Once Saved, Always Saved?* (New York: University Press of America, 2003), 47.

person's spiritual growth. Our misconception of sin can lead us to a misconception of grace, and a misconception of grace can lead us to a misconception of our purpose in life. Paul writes to Timothy that if we are dead in Christ, we will live with him and if we suffer for Christ, we will reign with Christ (2 Tim. 2:12). The problem arises when Christians refuse to die to the passions of this life and remain quiet when persecution comes, they forfeit the promise to live with Christ and reign with Christ. Does that mean they lose eternal life, absolutely not, but they lose the right of rulership. God's kingdom is of a master – slave model, as modeled in the parables; everyone reports to a boss. A slave may have eternal life, but what enjoyment is there to be on the bottom? In contrast, a ruler has praise and honor, which makes life enjoyable. This is portrayed by Jesus in the parable of the Wise and Foolish Virgins.

2.   A View of the Parable of the Ten Virgins

The Parable of the Ten Virgins is one of the most misunderstood teachings of Jesus. The greatest difficulty that the church over the centuries has had with this parable is the severe punishment meted out to the five virgins who did not have sufficient oil.

"Then shall the kingdom of heaven be likened unto ten virgins, which took their lamps, and went forth to meet the bridegroom. And five of them were wise, and five were foolish. They that were foolish took their lamps, and took no oil with them: But the wise took oil in their vessels with their lamps. While the bridegroom tarried, they all slumbered and slept. And at midnight there was a cry made, Behold, the bridegroom cometh; go ye out to meet him. Then all those virgins arose, and trimmed their lamps. And the foolish said unto the wise, Give us of your oil; for our lamps are gone out. But the wise answered, saying, Not so; lest there be not enough for us and you: but go ye rather to them that sell, and buy for yourselves. And while they went to buy, the bridegroom came; and they that were ready went in with him to the marriage: and the door was shut. Afterward came also the other virgins, saying, Lord, Lord, open to us. But he answered and said, Verily I say unto you, I know you not" (Matt. 25:1-12).

To understand this parable, you must have an understanding of its cultural background. The typical Jewish marriage custom began with the betrothal. Parents often chose a wife for their son, approaching the parents of the woman they desired to marry their son. If there is an agreement, the next step is to come to an agreement on the marriage present. This was not just a cute gift such as a lamp or a standard fee such as two cows, but a carefully calculated compensation gift from the groom to the family of the bride. People had children to care for them in their old age. Both sons and daughters contributed to the overall income of the family unit, therefore when a daughter is married, her income is lost to the family and there must be compensation. Since all parents have the highest regard for their daughters, they naturally expect the highest compensation for their daughter. Here is where the Friend of the Bridegroom steps in. He not only knows the groom very well, he also has a good knowledge of the bride. He is impartial in his assessment, noting both their strengths and weaknesses of character and if their personalities will be a good match. In our Western culture, we are told that opposites attract. However in Eastern cultures, for centuries, parents chose a wife for their son, or a husband for their daughter by very carefully selecting someone who was as close as match to their personality as possible. A introvert was not a match for an extrovert. A person who loved to laugh was not a match for a serious person. A person who was educated was not a match for someone not educated. With this knowledge, he negotiates a worth of the bride and when the two parties agree, the marriage gift is exchanged and the two families are linked. The second gift is the dowry. This is a gift from the father of the bride to the bride. In many ancient cultures, this was expensive jewelry she could not sell before her husband's death, or in the case of extreme poverty, the gift was designed to be a source of help in a dire time of need. The third gift, the bridegroom's gift, was from the groom to his bride, which often consisted of clothes and jewelry. With the contract sealed between the two families, the groom returns with the Friend of the Bridegroom to his father's house, who prepares a place for his son and new daughter-in-law to reside. Once the house is built, a feast is arranged and then he sends his son to go get his bride. The son always leaves in the evening and often arrives at the house of the bride late at night.

The Parable of the Marriage Feast tells us a significant amount about ancient Jewish marriage feasts (Matt. 22:1-14, Lk 14:16-24). Feasts were very important to the poor in ancient times. Though you had to be invited to get past the door and sit at a table to be fed, many were left outside the gate and were given the leftovers.

The role of lamps in the Ancient world is also important to understand. The lamps were large, dome-shaped torch that contained rags soaked in oil which slowly burned, allowing the person to walk with them in their hand outside. These lamps would last several hours before more oil was needed. The Greek word here is "lamtas", which means "torch".[168] However, the Greek word for "lamp" as used in a house is "luchnon" and is a smaller light set on a lamp stand (Matt. 5:15).[169] The Hebrews started their day at about 6:00 AM and ended it at about 6:00 PM, due to the amount of sunshine and because their days changed from one day to

168   Frederick Danker, *Greek-English Lexicon*. (Chicago: University of Chicago Press, 3rd. ed., 2000) 585

169   Ibid, Danker, 607.

another at 6:00 PM. Most battles and almost all travel were in daytime.

The Gospel of Matthew is the only Gospel that records the parable of the Wise and Foolish Virgins. The Gospel of Matthew is also the only gospel that records the teachings about the "kingdom of heaven", while the others speak only of the "kingdom of God". The difference is that the 'kingdom of God" represents the new kingdom Christ was establishing on earth, whereas the "kingdom of heaven" is strictly the eternal heavenly abode of God, his angels and his saints.

The Gospel of Matthew can be divided into 5 discourses, and this parable is located in the last discourse, which is about the return and judgment at the coming of the Son of Man. After Matthew records the words of Jesus warning about end time suffering (Matt. 24:4-13), the gospel preached in all nations (24:14), the coming great tribulation (24:15-28) and the second coming (24:29-31). Matthew now exhorts his readers to be watchful and prepared for the second coming with 5 parables: the Parable of the Homeowner, the Parable of the 2 Kinds of Servants, the Parable of the 10 Virgins, the Parable of the Talents and the Parable of the Sheep and Goats. These complete the teachings of Jesus and Matthew now closes his gospel with the last days of Jesus, his crucifixion and resurrection (Matt. 26-28).

Ellicott's Commentary suggests that the bride is the church and the members of the church are represented by the ten virgins. Five virgins have an outward life of holiness, who let their light shine before others but later when their lights grow dim they refill their lamps. The other five virgins do not have an outward life of holiness and, in their carelessness, let their lights burn out.[170] There are several problems with this interpretation. Firstly, it suggests that Christ is going to marry the institution called the church. Christ is coming to marry a bride, a woman who has proven herself worthy to be married to him, not some staunchy religious system. Secondly, if the ten virgins represent believers through the ages, even the five who were wise allowed their light to grow dim before the world. It is as if they had to repent of letting their light grow dim and did so by getting more oil, as if they had to go through a revival to awaken their love for the groom. The problem with the belief that "I know you not" and being shut out of the marriage generally has meant that they lost their salvation. As one of my theologians has commented, the penalty does not fit the crime. The other problem is if the ten virgins are the church, then only 50 percent of believers go to heaven. This contradicts the Lord's promise that, "If you shall confess with thy mouth the Lord Jesus, and shall believe in your heart that God hath raised him from the dead, you shall be saved" (Rom 10:9). Therefore, this theory has too many holes to be theologically sound.

---

170   Charles John Ellicott, *Ellicott's Bible Commentary*. (Grand Rapids: Zondervan Publishing, 1971), 742.

Wilkins argues that both the wise and the foolish virgins became drowsy and fell asleep.[171] If they represent the church, then it means Jesus was saying the church will fall asleep shortly before he comes again. I would argue that this is bad theology. Wilkins further argues that the treatment of the foolish virgins is a stark, straightforward statement of rejection of a person who does not have a true relationship with Jesus, resulting in their damnation. The problem here is that these women are virgins, that is, they have worked to keep themselves pure, which means that they indeed were in a true relationship with the groom. They did not want to do anything immoral to disqualify themselves to be called a virgin, or to do anything that would bring reproach on the groom. Their only mistake is that they had a lack of oil. These women, in the natural life of Israel, though they had missed this wedding, they still qualified as virgins and could be the attendants at another bride's wedding in the following weeks. Therefore, since Jesus is speaking to Israelites, they understood the qualifications and duties of the virgins and understood the necessity of being ready for the coming of the groom.

Clark agues that the five foolish virgins had hearts once illuminated by faith and love, but they have since back-slidden from the salvation of God. The light that once was in them became darkness, and they have not searched in

---

171   Michael Wilkins, *The New International Version Commentary on Matthew*. (Grand Rapids: Zondervan, 2004), 804.

time enough for a fresh supply of salvation.[172] Clark argues that the grace a person receives is just enough for their own soul, and you cannot borrow grace from another for your soul. The problem with this view is that it disjoints the body of Christ, one not able or willing to help another which contradicts 1 Cor 12:12-26, which teaches our interdependence on each other in the body of Christ.

Finis Dake argues that the parable does not represent the church because all Christians will go up in the rapture and will be at the marriage supper of the Lamb (1 Thes 4:16). The oil does not represent the Holy Ghost because the purpose of the Spirit baptism is for the endowment of power, not for saving the soul (Acts 1:4). Only those who are baptized by the Holy Spirit will go up in the rapture, while the rest go through the tribulation. There is only one kind of Christian, not two (1 Cor 5:17).[173] His arguments are compelling but his argument reduces the parable to a nice story, whereas Jesus is telling the story to warn his followers that there is a price to be paid to be faithful with corresponding eternal rewards.

The general belief that we go to heaven, that we are all part of the bride and are married to Jesus, and that we all get own very special mansion is much more wishful

---

172   Adam Clarke, *Clarke's Commentary* – Matthew – Acts, Vol 5. (New York: Abingdon Press, 1831), 238.

173   Finis Dake, *Dake's Annotated Reference Bible*. (Lawrenceville, Georgia: Dake Bible Publishing), 82.

thinking than what can be substantiated by scripture. There is a reward system for obedience. That is the underlying principle beneath these five parables, for if we will feed the hungry, give drink to the thirsty, clothe the naked or minister to those sick or in prison, there is a reward (Matt. 26:31-46). A person who accepts Christ shortly before death will not receive the rewards that a person who has labored for the gospel most of their life will. To argue that the thief on the cross will receive a mansion and come back to rule and reign with Christ is nonsense. If there are crowns to be earned, there are also mansions to be earned. This parable is situated in the middle of five similar parables that all speak of rewards according to one's deeds. If we all got the same rewards, there would be no need of a judgment, no one would be accountable for their deeds, and rewards would be meaningless, if they were all the same. Therefore, our rewards will be as unique as our faces, no person will receive the same rewards because no two people are the same.

Current Church trends also have impacted our current understanding of this parable. At the turn of the last century, after the Azusa Street Revival sparked the Pentecostal Movement, theologians came up with a new interpretation of what the Parable of the 10 Virgins meant. If the oil indeed represent being baptized with the fire and power of the Holy Ghost, then the five wise virgins are Christians who move in the gifts of the Holy Ghost whereas the five foolish virgins received the infilling of the Holy Ghost, but did not become baptized by the Holy Ghost, they rejected the evidence of speaking in tongues. One of most apparent problems with this theory is that there were so few Pentecostals a hundred years ago, and no one could imagine that it would represent 50 percent of the church. Today, we are much more informed about church growth. Today, there are more Christians alive than lived in the first 1,900 years of the church. The massive expansion in the last 40 years of Pentecostalism has made Pentecostals the second largest group in Christianity behind the Catholics. Current church trends suggest that by the year 2025, the growth of Pentecostalism will be so staggering that most Christians will be Pentecostal. Gary McGee, in his book on South American Missions, reports that between 1967 and 1987, the Pentecostal growth of South America was more than twice its population growth. The Pentecostals on Columbia grew 560 percent between 1960 and 1970. Since the Catholic Church considers a baptized infant as a member of the church until death, there are millions of Pentecostals in South America that have nothing to do with Catholicism, but are still counted as Catholics. So why do Pentecostals have such explosive growth? Coleman argues that shortcuts in evangelism have failed, that the costly principles of leadership development and reproduction seem to have been submerged beneath the easier strategy of mass recruitment, the nearsighted objective of popular recognition generally took precedence over the long-range goal of reaching the world. Well-intended ceremonies, programs, organizations, commissions and crusades of human ingenuity are trying valiantly to do a job that only can be done by men in the power of the Holy Spirit.[174] I agree with Coleman that so much of what the church does is by the mind and will of men, and not by the will of the Holy Spirit.

There is sufficient evidence to say that 50 percent of all Christians, since the time of Christ, will be spirit-filled, tongues-talking Christians by the time Christ returns. This, however, still leaves one two perplexing problems. Firstly, what happens to the 50 percent of the church that is represented by the foolish virgins? Secondly, what is meant by the bride? In recent years, there have been a number of individuals that have been lifted up into heaven and have written about they witnessed in heaven. One writer writes about how he met his former pastor in heaven, who with tears told how that he was destined to sit on one of the thrones that surround the throne of God. Yet he will spend eternity in the outer areas of heaven. As a pastor, he ruled his staff ruthlessly, often firing pastors for not meeting his growth targets. His zeal to build a megachurch was at the expense of hurting people under him. When he saw what he could have achieved with a gentile spirit and his loss of rewards, his only reaction was overwhelming grief and weeping. Other writers speak of heaven having many levels

---

174   Robert E. Coleman, *Master Plan of Evangelism*. (Michigan: Revell Books, 2010), 47.

and that higher levels were more glorious than lower levels. One writer speaks of how when he looked back at a lower level, it appeared as outer darkness, even though while he was at that level, it appeared like a nice day. I believe that the foolish virgins did not lose their salvation, but would go to an outer area of heaven where there is much less of the glory of God, and they wept bitterly for having lost what they were destined to have.

If then all the virgins go to heaven, what is significant about the bride? Like the other ten, she is a virgin, that is, morally pure. But she is specifically set apart because of her love for the groom. In natural life, only the bride loves the groom, the virgins are all waiting for their lover to come. In the parable, if all eleven represent the church, all eleven love the groom, Jesus. But it is the bride who alone is so compelled by love that she will do anything asked of her; she will cast the world aside just to be with him. As a spirit-filled Pentecostal for over 40 years, I have witnessed many Pentecostals that love Jesus; they have faith, good works and are morally upright. However, I have also witnessed these very same Pentecostals have a love for the world and are unwilling to live sacrificially for Christ. I believe that this parable, in fact, speaks of three kinds of Christians:

1) Spirit-filled believers who are so in love with Jesus that they live sacrificially to be a beacon of light and help to all around them.

2) Spirit-filled believers who love Jesus with a few conditions, though morally pure and have faith, their walk is not sacrificial. Their family or financial concerns come ahead of helping the needy.

3) Born-again believers who do not believe in being spirit-filled, who are morally pure and have faith, but religion is a duty and never a sacrifice.

If this is the right interpretation, then only one in eleven Christians (9 percent) will have the privilege of being married to Jesus. I believe it is these Christians who alone will come back and reign with Christ while the others will enjoy heaven, but with limited rewards. I am of the conviction that the parable speaks of the church as being represented by the bride and the ten virgins, meaning that one in eleven Christians marry Christ, five in eleven (45.5 percent) Christians witness the marriage, and the remaining five in eleven (45.5 percent) remain in heaven, but are shut out from the marriage feast. The parable clearly teaches that atonement was different for the bride than it was for the wise virgins and also different for the foolish virgins.

The message of Matthew was to exhort his readers to be watchful and prepared for the second coming. Matthew gives five parables that clearly teach us there are rewards to gain and rewards to lose. However, many pastors have been **guilty** of considering them not much more than Sunday School stories.

Chapter 14

THE IMPLICATIONS FOR TODAY'S CHURCH

I am under the conviction that the manner in which a church views sin has two impacts; how they will treat people in their faith community and how they will shape their future evangelistic endeavors. Carter argues that Jesus, nor Paul, condemned individuals simply because they missed the mark, yet it is ironic that many modern Christians would use selected teachings of Jesus and Paul to scrutinize fellow strugglers for the purpose of determining if they can accept them or not.[175] Jesus died for our sins, but we must bear the consequences of our sins. Sin does not prevent spiritual maturity, because it can be forgiven, but the consequence of sin often prevents spiritual maturity. Forgiveness often does not wipe away regret, and the consequences often injure our self-image. Often low self-image leads to low self-esteem, and low self-esteem often perpetuates a sense of unworthiness.

---

175   Les Carter, *Grace and Divorce: God's Healing Gift to Those Whose Marriages Fall Short.* (San Francisco: Wiley Printing, 2005), 14.

Unworthiness puts the believer out of the battle for souls and the church loses a soldier.

Regarding the future of the church, the Latter Rain Revival was prophesied by Smith Wigglesworth and Charles Price, who declared a two-part revival would occur in Canada, first in the late 1940s and then 50 years later, 10 times greater than the first revival. Not only did the 1947 revival happen, but many Canadian churches are poised to receive the second revival. In 1984, Paul Yongi Cho said the Lord told him that Canada would open the way for Jesus to return to earth. It is of little surprise that Satan has been working overtime in Canada in the last 30 years to defeat the Canadian Church, but he will not succeed. There are a number of things that the Church must watch as indicators of the imminent return of Christ, but what happens in Israel and the coming world-wide revival starting in Canada are foremost important. Rick Joyner writes of the vision he had of the church on May 11, 1992, where he saw a surfer overwhelmed by a large wave, which landed him in hospital. Yet with great resolve, he once more went to the beach, now healed and more muscular, with a bigger board, he walked past bodybuilders who were only there to show off their muscles, and was now ready for the big wave. Some churches will simply watch the coming wave of revival from the beach, others will be overwhelmed while a few will be ready. Overall, the church has not been taking practical steps to get ready for the coming revival.[176] It is a somber picture of the church, but it does not have to be; the church has an opportunity to re-evaluate its position on sin, because revival, by definition, means "to revive", and historically revivals turn people away from sin.

Bishop Bill Hamon has been instrumental in birthing The Prophetic Movement, The Apostolic Movement, the Saints Movement and the Third Reformation. This Third Reformation will be accompanied by the coming revival that will sweep millions into the Church and will give church organizations the freedom to significantly shift in new directions regarding the qualifications of membership.[177]

It is my conviction that if churches have so many wanting to join, the churches will no longer be scrapping among themselves for members and no longer accusing one another of "sheep-stealing". Barriers that separate will fall as churches realize that they will need to share resources to meet the need. The Church will emerge with a level of unity never seen before, and churches will no longer need to accept people with immoral lifestyles. This Third Reformation will have two components, holiness and equipping the saints to evangelize the world. Does that mean the churches will

---

176   Rick Joyner, "The Next Wave is Upon Us", *Morning Star Journal*, Vol. 2, No. 4, (1992), 30-32.

177   Bill Hamon, *Apostles, Prophets, And the Coming Moves of God*, (Shippensburg, PA: Destiny Image Publishers, 1997), 11.

abandon those that have committed an unpardonable sin? Absolutely not! Hope remains. However, just as sheep were led to the pastures by the shepherd that he might protect them in the day and then to the sheep fold at night, that they would be protected at night; in the same, the church must protect its members. I am under the conviction that there will arise independent religious organizations that will specialize in restoring people bound in these evils. Just as Alcoholics Anonymous provides hope for alcoholics, so other organizations can provide healing for those having had an abortion, for those caught in adultery, homosexuality, witchcraft, prostitution or cults. Rather than just offer counseling, they can teach salvation and lead the person through to salvation. Once they have proven real change, then the organization can introduce them into a church and the church can be confident that these newcomers will not prey on other believers or contaminate other believers. I have personally witnessed church leaders committing things they should not do. Deacons have been criminally charged and sent to jail. Pastors have been warned by the Holy Spirit to change their behavior, but they did not change and suddenly went to an early grave. Some denominations consider divorce so evil that the divorced person has no opportunity to be involved in the church, yet other men who have a reputation for shady business deals are made deacons. Divorce is not and never has been an unpardonable sin. Just as there are holiness qualifications for leaders, there will come holiness qualifications for membership.

Opponents of the Church have learned that there is no greater weapon to destroy the Church than by use of the courts. In Canada, the gay and abortion communities have forced the courts to declare it is now a criminal act for a Christian minister to speak against homosexuals or abortionists. Yet the church must take a stand. I believe as a result of this study, that a Christian who becomes a homosexual violates their salvation covenant. Many Christian ministers believe there is no such thing as a "Christian Homosexual", just as there is no such thing as a "Christian Abortionist" or a "Christian Witch". The three religions of Islam, Hinduism and Buddhism, are so different that there is no such thing as an "Islamic Hindu" or an "Islamic Buddhist". That is not an attack on their religion, but a mere reality that all religions are exclusive in their membership; if you do not agree with the ideology of the religion, you are not welcome. To say there is no such thing as a "Christian Homosexual" is not an attack on their lifestyle, they can do anything they want to do lawfully, but they cannot call themselves Christians. I am aware there are homosexual churches whose attendees believe they are Christians, but the reality is that they are misled just like people who once believed the world was flat. The sad fact is that these homosexuals and abortionists at death will be cast away from Christ; but then it will be too late to repent. The church will always offer help to homosexuals so they can leave that lifestyle, but admission into a church must come with identifiable proof of a changed lifestyle.

Church history has clearly shown a link between holiness and revival. Church history, beginning with the Seven Churches of Revelation, has proven again and again a church lasts only a generation after it has lost its holiness. Church growth by lowering ethical standards, so as to accept anyone into a church, is flawed. The leaning tower of Pisa, Italy, is famous. However, the tower is really a bell tower for the cathedral and beside the cathedral is the baptistery building. A person had to take classes and prove they understood the fundamentals of the Catholic church before they could be water baptized by immersion. Only after baptism could they then enter the cathedral and receive communion.

Most Christians have a smorgasbord of beliefs. They pick up some ideas from TV evangelists, some other ideas from religious books and some from their local church. Many cannot correctly explain the fundamentals of the church they belong to. Many others search for churches that impose the least ethical or moral standards; and merely occasionally attend a church for friendships, entertainment or to appease a **guilty** conscience.

The purpose of a church is not to sugarcoat the gospel or give people an appeasement for their sins. The purpose of the church is to bring healing to people spiritually, emotionally and relationally. Healing never works outside the context of holiness.

Chapter 15

CONCLUSION

T his book began as a quest to better understand what constituted sin. A few years ago, while developing a paper in seminary on Hebrews, I became frustrated that I could not find a clear, concise definition of sin. In my research, I have learned immensely. I have been provoked by what I discovered, and I have had to readjust my personal convictions regarding sin. My starting point was my original thesis that a church's fundamental understanding of the concept of sin impacted their members' spiritual life and social interaction, as their choices influence for both good and evil both within and without the church environment, affecting the very destiny of the church.

It is common knowledge that believers learn what is expected of them when they hear a sermon, because the purpose of a sermon is to provoke believers to godliness. In order to do that, the sermon must set clear guidelines as to what is unacceptable conduct, and unacceptable conduct is framed by an understanding of sin. Therefore, as the believer makes choices that impact their spiritual walk, they in turn impact their family, their community, their workplace and their church fellowship. Since churches are a reflection of their members, both the level of godliness and the attitudes of sin impact the direction and ultimate destiny of the church. An example is the Salvation Army, a church that began as a temperance movement and today still ministers to the alcoholic. The Salvation Army, therefore, framed a movement around their opposition to one sin, alcoholism. However, the Church must move beyond being in opposition to this or that sin, rather if it can grasp a true concept of how Moses, Jesus and the disciples understood the concept of sin, its very destiny will be affected.

I have shown there are a number of problems that contributed to a skewed view of sin. The Hebrews used very specific words to define concepts of sin, yet today the word sin is used as a super word to include any and all wrong.

Historically, the Early Church Fathers had to believe in the Son of God when society demanded they worship Caesar as god in the flesh, masters had total control over their slaves, even for sexual exploitation, and had to wrestle with those who denied their faith to save their lives. In Medieval times, the church developed the theory of purgatory to put the fear of God into believers. The Reformers restructured major doctrines and, in their zeal, killed other believers who did not believe as they did. Some Reformers depicted former Popes in hell, whereas other Reformers banned anyone from their community who did not adhere to their strict rule of conduct. The Age of Enlightenment would spawn a wide range of theological beliefs including restricted diets, multiple marriages and denials of the existence of hell. The Modern Church would rise up in opposition to the sins of socialism, communism, liberalism and rationalism. This age began with fiery sermons of fire and damnation, yet the fear remains that the Modern Church age may end with little conviction of sin.

Few theologians study original languages anymore, meaning pastors often teach from translations that are flawed. When theological teachers produce flawed commentaries, and denominations grasp as tightly as they ever have to their favorite traditions, the ability to accept biblical concepts of sin becomes increasingly more difficult, resulting in society defining what sin should be and not the church.

The Hebrew scriptures are very clear regarding unpardonable sins, for there was no sacrifice for these sins, just stoning. The sin of apostasy consisted of a repudiation of the Law of Moses and turning away to other gods. Paul, likewise, warned of those would repudiate and turn from the gospel to fables. The sin of evilness had a violent component, where people terrorized others for their own gain. Christ called demons evil spirits, because of their destructive violent nature. Paul speaks of lewd, evil men who wanted to kill him because he preached the gospel and instructed the church to judge evil men, and not allow them to enter the church, for the protection of the believers. The sin of wickedness consists of those who are lawless. The sin of abomination means to defile that which is holy in a non-violent manner. It includes those who or participate in witchcraft, homosexuality and oppression of the poor. Jesus condemned those who committed abomination, because they justified their actions in their own eyes.

The forgivable sins had a corresponding sacrifice, so that a repentant violator of the Law could be forgiven and be restored. The Lord makes provision for sins committed ignorantly. Shortcomings, or missing the mark, are sins that occur when a person misses his way, sins often done by mistake but without a sense of malicious intent. This is the most common word for sin in the NT, and there are numerous verses that state that Christ died for the short-comings of people. The sin of rebellion is a direct violation of well-understood requirements of the law, or other cove-nants or agreements. Paul spoke of rebellion as despising the government of God. The sin of perversion, or iniquity, is to twist the truth. Eli's sons offered strange fire, they perverted what was clearly defined a sacrificial protocol. Jesus talks of tares among the wheat, those that look like wheat but are imposters. The sacrifices for these sins were dependent on the seriousness of the offense and, except for the poor, there was no relation between the wealth of a person and the value of the sacrifice.

The court adjudicated sins were offenses between people that judges made the final verdict of guilt or innocence. The sin of injustice involved using false weights and volumes, refusal to honor debt pledges and usury. Jesus spoke of being faithful in unrighteous mammon. The sin of treachery involved deceit and faithlessness to a covenant. Paul speaks of the treachery of covenant-breakers. The sin of offense is a breaking of the Law in such a way that it causes an uproar in the entire community, a contamination of normal life.

The theology for today, that is the application of these sin concepts, clearly points to the conclusion that while Christ died for all people, that no one is exempt from accepting salvation, nevertheless there remains limited atonement for some sins. This would appear a paradox, but the belief that Christ died for every sin is also a paradox in that it does away for the need of judgment. I have come to the conclusion that anyone who believes on the name of Christ enters the Kingdom of God, however profession of faith does not eliminate responsibility or consequences. The Lord has restored the ministry of deliverance to the Body to strip away the evil spiritual authority passed down from generations, and to destroy the power of evil oaths people have entered into. Sonship, however, requires obedience to a higher standard that most churches today are not willing to enforce. Many churches are **guilty** of compromise in the hopes of gaining memberships. Yet even believers can commit deadly sins that have eternal consequences.

It is my conviction that the implications of my research for today's church are far reaching. The church is now entering the Third Reformation that will see the greatest days of the Church, days of incredible miracles and revival. These will be days when churches will no longer be fighting over sheep, but will share resources because the need will be so great. A call to holiness will mean churches will have the opportunity to heighten their admission standards. Independent organizations can minister to those who have committed unforgivable sins, so that the churches are protected from predators or those who contaminate. The biblical model is clear, there are unforgivable sins, however God is the only judge and he alone chooses to whom he will have mercy. It is not about a single act but a lifestyle. If the Protestant Church is faithful to recognize these unpardonable sins, ministers will no longer be **guilty** of teaching that Jesus forgives every sin.

BIBLIOGRAPHY

Alcorn, Randy, *Christians in The Wake of the Sexual Revolution.* Portland, Oregon: Multnomah Press, 1985.

Blum, Howard, *The Gold of Exodus.* New York, Simon & Schuster, 1998.

Bonar, Andrew, *A Commentary on the Book of Leviticus.* Grand Rapids: Baker Books, 1978

Bowen, Barbara, *Strange Scriptures that Perplex the Western Mind.* Eerdmans, Grand Rapids,1987.

Braun, Michael, *Second Class Christians.* Dowers Grove, Illinois: InterVarsity Press, 1989.

Bromiley, Geoffrey W., *Historical Theology: An Introduction.* Grand Rapids, Eerdmans, 1978.

Brown, F, and S. Driver and C. Briggs, *The Brown-Driver-Briggs Hebrew and English Lexicon.* Peabody, Mass.: Hendrickson, 2003.

Bruce, F.F., *The Hard Sayings of Jesus.* Downers Grove, Illinois: InterVarsity Press, 1983.

Bruner, Frederick, *Matthew: A Commentary.* Grand Rapids: Eerdmans, 2004.

Carnell, Edward J., *An Introduction to Christian Apologetics.* Grand Rapids, Eerdmans, 1948.

Carter, Les, *Grace and Divorce: God's Healing Gift to Those Whose Marriages Fall Short.* San Francisco: Wiley Printing, 2005.

Claybrook, Frederick, *Once Saved, Always Saved?* New York: University Press of America, 2003.

Clarke, Adam, *Clarke's Commentary*, vol 1. Nashville: Abingdon Press, 1836.

Coleman, Robert E., *Master Plan of Evangelism.* Michigan: Revell Books, 2010,

Dake, Finis Jennings, *Dake's Annotated Reference Bible.* Lawrenceville, Georgia: Dake Bible Sales, 1963.

Danker, Frederick William, *A Greek-English Lexicon of the New Testament and other Early Christian Literature*, 3d ed, Chicago: University of Chicago, 2000.

Doorly, William, *Prophet of Love: Understanding the Book of Hosea.* New York: Paulist Press, 1991.

Duty, Guy, *God's Covenants and Our Time.* Minneapolis. Minnesota: Bethany Fellowship Printing, 1964.

Ellicott, Charles John, *Ellicott's Bible Commentary.* Grand Rapids: Zondervan Publishing, 1971.

Elwell, Walter A., *Baker Theological Dictionary of the Bible.* Grand Rapids: Baker Books, 1996.

Erickson, Millard, *Christian Theology.* Grand Rapids: Baker Books, 2000.

Feinberg, John S., *Continuity and Discontinuity.* Westchester, Illinois: Crossway Books, 1988.

Finegan, Jack, *Handbook of Biblical Chronology.* New Jersey: Princeton University Press, 1964.

Gaglardi, Maureen, *The Path of the Just*, Vol. 2. Vancouver: New West Press, 1971.

Gonzalez, Justo, *The Story of Christianity*, Vol. 1. The Early Church to the Dawn of The Reformation, San Francisco: Harper Collins Publishers, 1984.

Gonzalez, Justo *The Story of Christianity*, Vol. 2. The Reformation to the Present Day, New York: Harper Collins Publishers, 1985.

Gruits, Patricia Beall, *Understanding God.* Detroit, Michigan: Whitaker Books, 1972.

Gunkel, Hermann, *Genesis.* Gottingen: 1910.

Haldeman, I.M., *The Tabernacle Priesthood and Offerings.* New Jersey: Fleming Revell Company, 1925.

Hamon, Bill, *Apostles, Prophets, And the Coming Moves of God.* Shippensburg, PA: Destiny Image Publishers, 1997.

Henry, Carl F. H., ed., *Baker's Dictionary of Christian Ethics.* Grand Rapids: Baker Books, 1973.

Hillerbrand, Hans, *The Reformation.* Grand Rapids: Baker Books, 1972.

Hughes, P.E., *Commentary on the Epistle to the Hebrews.* Grand Rapids: Eerdmans, 1977.

Joyner, Rick, *"The Next Wave is Upon Us"*, Morning Star Journal, Vol. 2, No. 4, 1992.

Kelly, Geoffrey, "The Life and Death of a Modern Martyr," Christianity Today, (Issue 32, Vol. 10, No. 4).

Kylstra, Chester and Betsy, *Restoring the Foundations.* Henderson, NC: Proclaiming His Word Publications, 2001.

Ladd, George, *A Theology of the New Testament.* Grand Rapids: Eerdmans, 1974.

Macquarrie, John, *Dictionary of Christian Ethics.* Philadelphia: Westminster Press, 1967).

McGrath, Alister, *The Christian Theology Reader.* Lexicon Oxford, England: Blackwell Publishers, 2000.

Moe, Kenneth Alan, *The Pastor's Survival Guide.* Bethesda, MD: Alban Institute Publication, 2001.

Packer, J.J., *Fundamentalism and the Word of God.* Grand Rapids: Eerdmans Publishing, 1958.

Pratico, Gary, and Miles Van Pelt, *Basics of Biblical Hebrew Grammar.* Grand Rapids, Zondervan, 2001.

Rae, Scott, *Moral Choices.* Grand Rapids, Zondervan Publishing, 1995.

Robinson, H. Wheeler, *Inspiration and Revelation in the Old Testament*, Oxford: Oxford Press, 1964.

Rouselle, Aline*, Porneia: On Desire and the Body in Antiquity.* Oxford: Basel Blackwell Inc., 1988.

Smith, Mark, *The Early History of God.* San Francisco, Harper & Row Publishers, 1990).

Thiessen, Henry, *Lectures in Systematic Theology.* Grand Rapids: Eerdmans, 1979.

Turner, David, L., *Baker Theological Dictionary of the Bible.* Walter A. Elwell, ed., Grand Rapids: Baker Books, 1996.

Wilkins, Michael, *The New International Version Commentary on Matthew*, Grand Rapids: Zondervan, 2004.

CPSIA information can be obtained
at www.ICGtesting.com
Printed in the USA
LVHW04s1057091018
592864LV00002B/2/P